Smarketing™
Sell Smarter, Not Harder.

by

Peter Strohkorb, CiMM, GAICD

Copyright © 2022 Peter Strohkorb

All rights reserved.

DEDICATIONS

This book is dedicated to all hard-working business leaders, executives, and sales and marketing professionals everywhere.

After all, without you, no business could exist.

My vision is for a world where Sales and Marketing support each other to be the very best they can be, and to achieve the best possible outcomes for your business, for its customers, and for the individuals involved.

When you successfully implement Smarketing into your organization, your customers will enjoy their buying experience, it will make them keep coming back to do more business with you, and they will become raving advocates who refer more business to you.

I hope you will enjoy reading my book, and that it encourages you to consider introducing Smarketing into your organization.

I am available to support you with my advice and guidance. Please just ask.

ACKNOWLEDGMENTS

This book would not have been possible without input from some very kind specialists in their respective fields. My heartfelt gratitude goes out to them for their expert insight and generous support:

Donal Daly, Donal Daly, Chief Rocket Launcher, 6 Rockets, and former Founder and CEO at Altify
Jodie Sangster, Chief Marketing Officer, IBM
Tiffani Bova.Global Global customer Growth and Innovation Evangelist, Salesforce.com, USA
Sonya Walker, Executive Vice President Cloud Strategic Growth and Sales Leader, Global Business Services, IBM
Rob Malkin, Vice President ANZ, Lifesize, Asia Pacific
Dr David Cooke, Managing Director at Konica Minolta Business Solutions Australia & New Zealand
David Duncan, Managing Director at SICK AG Asia Pacific
Gerhard Gschwandtner, Founder and CEO at Selling Power Magazine and Sales 3.0 Conferences, USA

A special "Thank You" also to:

Vanessa Strohkorb, my beautiful wife for her enduring support
John Michell for his kind hospitality and sanctuary
Bryan Szabo my excellent editor
Sandra Fernandez my ingenious graphic designer
Paul and Linda Croft for their book printing expertise and kind help

"Never mind a book about how to change myself. I need a book about making everyone else change."

TABLE OF CONTENTS

Preface: What is Smarketing? 15

Chapter 1: The Smarketing Philosophy 19

Chapter 2: The Smarketing Mindset 25

Chapter 3: Time to Go Smarketing 33

Chapter 4: The Many Business Benefits of Smarketing 39

Chapter 5: The Top 7 Smarketing Mistakes 61

Chapter 6: Measuring Smarketing Maturity 75

Chapter 8: Smarketing and the Sales Funnel 97

Chapter 9: The Smarketing Approach to Sales Lead Management 103

Chapter 10: Common Smarketing Implementation Roadblocks 109

Chapter 11: Smarketing and The Productivity Trinity 117

Chapter 12: Implementing Smarketing 129

Chapter 13: Various Client Success Stories 155

Chapter 14: Prevention is Better Than Cure 167

Chapter 15: Over to You Now, A Call to Action 171

Contact: 174

About the Author 175

Executive Foreword by Donal Daly

Serial Entrepreneur, Founder & Former CEO, Altify

There are few distinct viewpoints in business that are as polarized as those of marketing and sales professionals. Marketing is glamorous, sales is less so. Sales are measurable, marketing less so. The uneasy relationship between sales and marketing is widespread and infects almost all types of businesses, particularly technology companies that provide high value solutions to large corporations. Marketing folks decry the poor sales conversion rate delivered by the sales team, who in turn abhor what they would characterize as the risible value delivered by expensive marketing campaigns.

Throughout my career, I, like Peter, have interacted many sales and marketing professionals. The polarity of perspective is striking. "Salespeople are just quick-talking, quota-driven snake oil dealers" was the cant of the marketing quarter, while the sales constituency responded, "Sales draw the picture and marketing color it in!"

Like many opposing forces, however, their true interdependence is understated and sometimes unclear. The strategic marketing function (not marketing communications) believes that it sets out the game-plan, sometimes only to find that there are no players who understand the strategy. Sales execute plays, without understanding where the corporate goal is.

Today, the winners in both camps understand that success is only measured by successful customer engagements. On today's playing field, successful selling, and the leading sales professional, encapsulates the best of strategic marketing, but at an individual customer level. That demands collaboration with marketing. Today's marketing winners eschew their previous role as vehicles for value communication and take responsibility for value creation, delivered to carefully chosen prospects – to convert them into customers.

They need the perspective of the salesperson to fully inform that approach. Both now need to participate wholly in Smarketing – as defined and outlined by Peter here in this book. Sales and marketing can't afford to ignore each other in today's hyper-competitive markets.

Principles, once seemingly engraved in stone, now reveal themselves to be more fluid than rigid. In a world where 'value creation' is a necessity, and the foundation upon which profitable customer relationships are built, discrete activities conducted separately by sales and marketing, no longer suffices. The adage of 'it is all a numbers game' rings hollow in a world where information is everywhere, and customers are frequently as knowledgeable as you are about your products, and those of your competitor. Unless sellers and marketers together create – rather than just communicate – value, customers will look elsewhere.

Professional sales and marketing have evolved beyond a "Go get 'em, Tiger!" approach, and a good team listener will beat a fast talker anytime.

Customers don't distinguish any longer between sales and marketing. They now look to business professionals acting in concert to be their partners in developing a future vision for their organizations. They expect insight and actions – not just words.

I welcome Peter's continuous focus on the issue of Sales and Marketing collaboration. It is this formula that helps customers to succeed, and that is the goal that drives the best sales and marketing professionals.

- Donal Daly

Executive Foreword by Sonya Walker

Executive Vice President Cloud Strategic Growth and Sales Leader Global Business Services, IBM

For the last few decades, I have worked in international technology companies such as IBM, Infor, Oracle, SAP and SAS across all industries and am dedicated to helping my clients be successful. In this time, I have experienced a perplexing problem that has been allowed to develop in the business world, one that 'Smarketing' will solve.

We all know that the sales and marketing portfolios in organizations directly impact company revenue, overall financial performance, market share and profitability. Yet, they have evolved on divergent paths to the point that they have different C-level leaders, key performance indicators (KPIs), scorecards and financial metrics to measure success. In many instances, they operate in separate silos with competing interests, where at best they operate in a collegiate relationship and at worst they are divorced parties producing lackluster performance. They are separately lost in a competitive struggle for political relevance and executive recognition, being reactive to competitors and market forces when they should instead be high-performing teams proactively collaborating to drive superior results.

Imagine if all the effort and needless financial expenditure spent on competing internally within an organization were expended on fruitful collaboration that focuses all sales and marketing resources on customer outcomes, on winning more deals and on growing the business. I have implemented this solution whereby Sales and marketing teams come together (Smarketing), respect and benefit from each other's skills, inform, collaborate and evolve. They bring agility and speed to an organization and in doing so everybody wins.

Smarketing is not just good business – it is smart business!

I recommend Peter's book as a wakeup call to transform the often-unproductive relationship between Sales and Marketing teams in many organizations. This approach will empower your business with agility to respond to market forces, teams that can develop innovative campaigns and products and services that are truly customer centric.

The book provides excellent advice, clear guidance, a real framework and a proven methodology that, together, can contribute to sustainable success in terms of higher revenue, more profit, increased market share, improved customer satisfaction, better employee experience and superior brand reputation.

CEOs, Sales Leaders, Marketing Leaders and Executives everywhere should strongly consider Smarketing for their organization. Uniting, harmonizing, and solidifying your two most customer-facing resources for accelerated growth makes compelling sense.

Use this book as a catalyst for positive change and for winning results in your organization.

- Sonya Walker
Strategic Growth and Sales Leader, IBM

Executive Foreword by Jodie Sangster

Chief Marketing Officer - ANZ, IBM

Throughout my career I have experienced organizations where sales and marketing have worked well together, and others where they have not.

More often than not, it's the customer experience that suffers first, then the sales results, and then the employee experience.

All that is avoidable.

However, it is easy to see how the disconnect between Sales, Marketing and Customer Experience develops and, in many instances it is far more pervasive than business leaders like to acknowledge.

As Sales and Marketing professionals, it is essential that we solve this challenge. I

In this book, Peter shows that positive alignment and healthy collaboration of Sales and Marketing teams with their ideal Customers produces superior results.

There is money in getting Smarketing right.

Using this book, you can understand how to leverage the Smarketing concept, why it is important, and how to bring it into your organization and embed it into the fabric.

To me, Smarketing makes a lot of sense, it is quite simply what all Marketers and Sales Leaders should practice maximizing their revenue and market share. I recommend you read Peter's book

- Jodie Sangster
CMO ANZ, IBM

An Open Invitation

Dear Reader,

Thank you for your interest in this important subject matter and in this, my second book. After publishing my first book, The OneTEAM Method™, I realized that not every organization is ready to accept that Sales and Marketing can do better in supporting each other and their Customers to mutual benefit.

To their own detriment, this denial continues to hold many organizations back from boosting their sales performance and from accelerating their growth.

If only they knew that Smarketing is easy to implement.

You start with a simple online self-assessment at peterstrohkorb.com/smarketing-test

Then, Smarketing can be applied to just a single sales pursuit, e.g. a "must-win" deal, or to retain a key account.

Smarketing can also be used to streamline your entire revenue process, right through from sales lead generation to transaction and on to post-sales service and support.

To me, that illustrates the compelling nature of Smarketing.

Please feel free to reach out to me personally to discuss your specific situation, and to uncover how Smarketing can support your success.

I look forward to speaking with you.

Peter Strohkorb

Preface: What is Smarketing?

Unfortunately, it is now common to see fewer than 30% of sales reps achieve their sales quota. At the same time, sales cycles lengthen, prospects are becoming harder to reach, and buyers have a seemingly infinite choice of vendors.

It is time to rethink the way we sell. How can we achieve more?

My new book answers this question and outlines my proven methodology that leverages your existing resources to significantly boost sales performance across the board. Smarketing is a proven method that really boosts sales results.

In fact, it does more than that. However, it's the boost to top line revenue that usually grabs executives' initial attention.

Aside from boosting sales revenue though, Smarketing also aids operational productivity, lifts employee engagement and enhances customer experience. I will expand on these points later in this book.

For now, however, allow me to outline my rationale behind Smarketing.

In my opinion, to put it simply, the role of Marketing should be to draw potential new customers to your business and to your brand. In other words, to turn Suspects into Prospects.

So, the role of Marketing should be to help Sales to sell more. I say that:

Marketing exists to create an environment where sales can occur.

The role of Sales then is to take over these Prospects, to engage them and to guide them to transaction. They should be two sides of the same coin, two teams that work in unison towards a common goal.

At least that is the theory. I find though, that the reality is less harmonious and less clear-cut than the theory suggests:

Marketing often complains that their efforts are not appreciated by Sales.

Sales often complains that Marketing is not supporting them to achieve their sales quota.

But it is the Customer who often feels this disconnect the most.

If this situation is allowed to continue unchecked, the two functions will drift further and further apart. Things may become personal when each side starts talking more **about** the other, than **to** them.

You end up with a situation where Sales and Marketing retreat into separate silos, leading to an unharmonious work environment that tolerates under-performance and low productivity.

It doesn't have to be that way.

Smarketing restores the high levels of productivity that each function deserves and which they should receive from each other:

Sales + Marketing = Smarketing

Sales helps Marketing to better understand what Sales needs to be successful. Marketing will respond by better supporting the sales objectives. The customer will have a more consistent and enjoyable buying experience.

Everybody wins.

Smarketing boils down to doing more with existing resources, providing a classical productivity boost to your two most customer-facing functions and to your sales pipeline, resulting in sustainable sales revenue growth.

It may not be the old "Do more with less", but, at the very least, it is "Do better with what you already have".

The outcome is likely to be higher win rates, elevated revenue and profits, more accurate forecasting, happier employees and more satisfied customers.

Who would not want to be associated with that sort of success?

I hope you enjoy reading this book.

Please don't hesitate to reach out to me directly, I look forward to hearing from you.

Peter Strohkorb

Chapter 1:
The Smarketing Philosophy

The dictionary defines 'philosophy' thus:

Philosophy

fi 'lo sə fi

Noun

1. the study of the fundamental nature of knowledge, reality and existence, especially when considered as an academic discipline

2. the theory or attitude that acts as a guiding principle for behavior

When I use the term 'philosophy' I do so according to the second definition above. I mean philosophy as a guiding principle. The philosophy that animates Smarketing is the belief that teams working together towards a common outcome is far better than individuals working independently and hoping that it will all somehow come together in the end.

In other words, teamwork is better than isolation; collaboration is better than silo-fication.

The phrase "hope is not a strategy," attributed to former New York City Mayor Rudy Giuliani, really applies in this context.

We want – indeed, we need – more than just hope, we want results.

What sort of results and outcomes do we want?

Financial Results

Of course, being in business means that we want positive financial results, such as revenue and profit growth. We also want to deliver value to our shareholders. These results are measured in the monetary terms of dollars and cents.

External Recognition

We also want less-tangible results in the form of such things as customer satisfaction, customer advocacy and loyalty, brand profile and thought leadership. Being less tangible, they are harder to measure, but there are techniques available that can help us to understand how well, or poorly, we are doing in this respect.

Internal Recognition

In addition to the two above, we also want our employees to be happy and engaged in our business. We want them to be good ambassadors for our organization and enjoy a high level of job satisfaction. Often, we measure these results in terms of Employee Net Promoter Score or ENPS.

Peter Drucker famously said that "What gets measured, gets managed."

It also seems perfectly logical that we measure these three very different aspects in their own discrete ways. Equally logical is that we assign achievement targets and key performance indicators (KPIs) to each one. Thus, we are putting measurable focus on the teams that are charged with pursuing the above results.

The challenge is that in many organizations the KPIs that apply to Sales are not aligned with the KPIs for Marketing (and vice versa). Consequently, Sales and Marketing can become inward-focused and the communication channels between them can become blocked up. It is time to end this siloed approach and find a new and better way.

This is where the philosophy behind Smarketing comes in.

The changing habits of Buyers have necessitated a change to the way that organizations manage the interactions between their Sales and Marketing resources. These two teams need to work together as one, identifying and striving together to reach a common goal.

A Smarketing-first approach creates a constructive feedback loop that not only opens the bi-directional channels of communication, but it creates certain inter-dependencies for Sales and Marketing to collaborate more effectively.

This feedback loop is so critically important to me that it is even reflected in my business logo. The two arcs, representing Sales and Marketing respectively, come together to form a collaborative circle. Tellingly a circle made of gold.

I love it for its simplicity and the deep and powerful meaning that lies behind it for me.

Smarketing allows individual team members to play a part in the overall development of the solution, which means it gives them personal buy-in and a sense of shared purpose That ensures there will be little resistance when it comes to implementing Smarketing.

This buy-in takes place much earlier and at a much deeper level than it would if Smarketing were imposed from above.

It sets the teams up for true collaboration in the spirit of Smarketing. As is so often the case, the simplest solutions are often the most effective, and so it is with Smarketing as the essence of Smarketing is very simple and easy to understand:

Sales supports Marketing. And Marketing supports Sales.

Consequently:

Sales brings in more deals.

Marketing is recognized for its contribution to revenue.

Customers enjoy a superior experience.

Everybody wins!

Chapter Takeaway

The philosophy behind Smarketing is based on the fundamental belief that working in collaboration is better than working in isolation, that superior collaboration delivers superior results. We then discussed what these results should look like and touched on the causes of low Smarketing in sales organizations today.

One would think that Smarketing is axiomatic and that it should be the norm. The power to make this a reality in your business is in your hands.

Contact me if you would like help getting started right.

Peter Strohkorb

Chapter 2:
The Smarketing Mindset

Anyone in business knows that the ways of doing business have undergone tremendous change over the last few decades. It seems that everything is speeding up or being disrupted, and that nothing remains the same.

Businesses of all sizes and persuasions are finding it a challenge to keep up with the rate and the impact of change. Disruption is everywhere.

Yes, we now live in a VUCA world.

The way that Sellers interact with Buyers has not been immune from change. The increasing proliferation of digital platforms and sales channels alone has created immense complexity. Then consider the juxtaposition of business growth through international expansion and globalization, whilst needing to retain local legal and regulatory compliance, and you can give yourself a headache.

What is a CEO, or a business leader supposed to focus on first?

The natural temptation is to wrest back control of their business by turning all their attention inwards.

Alas, this is a fallacy.

It is the exact opposite that is required:

There has never been a time when organizations have needed to be more focused on their customers and on their prospects than today.

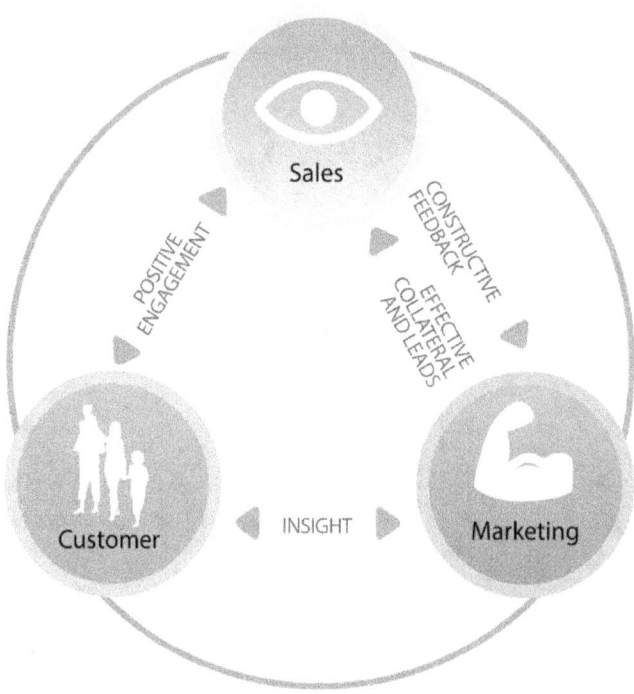

The image above illustrates the positive inter-relation that Smarketing enables between Sales, Marketing and Customers

It's what I call *"The Virtuous Circle of Collaboration"*:

If you want to drive sales growth AND improve customer experience, then your customer messaging needs to be consistent and value-creating across all your organization's customer touch points. And:

Your customer experience needs to live up to the expectations that your marketing messaging creates.

Think about it, what are the two most revenue-generating functions in your business? Right: It's not two separate functions at all. Instead, if you are doing Smarketing right, it will be your reinvigorated Sales and Marketing team that will deliver the results.

What does the solution look like?

We need to stop looking at our organizations from the inside-out. Instead, we need to start viewing our business from our customers' perspective, view it from the outside-in.

Here is how it works:

1. Daily, your salespeople have direct interactions with the market. They witness responses to marketing efforts and sales material. In a Smarketing-enabled organization they capture this direct insight and share it with their marketing counterparts.

2. Feedback from the sales force is highly valuable to Marketing to help finesse marketing messaging, website content, white papers, reports, and sales collateral and to make it even more immediately relevant to your target audience.

3. This, in turn, enables the sales force to strike more meaningful dialogues with their Customers and Prospects, lifting their sales conversations and equipping them with the means to close more deals, faster.

4. Last, not least, your customers benefit, because they enjoy a more meaningful and value-enhancing buying experience when

dealing with your salespeople, with your brand and with your organization.

So, what is the most effective way to achieve the desired business results?

As far back as 2014, Bain & Company summed up the changing landscape very aptly in their report, called "Mastering The New Reality of Sales"

https://www.bain.com/insights/mastering-the-new-reality-of-sales

- The line between Sales and Marketing will disappear; an integrated function will emerge to synchronize coverage and resources with target customers.

- Without a deliberate effort to reverse creeping complexity and administrative burden selling costs will grow faster than revenue.

- Prospects will have screened you out of consideration based on your digital footprint (or its absence) even before one of your representatives has a chance to understand their needs.

- Your customers will spend more time analyzing your offerings than you will on analytics to understand their buying behavior.

- A competitor will offer your customers better, more seamless service through lower-touch, lower-cost channels, winning share and loyalty.

- You will be forced to either retrain or turn over more than half of your reps to keep up with competitor sellers who truly add value, rather than just communicate features, and take orders.

It seems that many organizations are still finding adapting to these changes a daily challenge. Even worse, they often are hamstrung by short-term decision-making, shrinking budgets and entrenched personal perceptions and attitudes.

As a result, many organizations are seeking ways to enable more sales success through more effective collaboration between their sales and marketing teams.

Unfortunately, many still address this objective with short-term "Band-Aid" solutions or technology and apps, such as CRM systems, lead management software and collaboration tools.

Unfortunately, these just never seem to deliver sustainable business benefits and as overnight miracle cures the shine has come off them.

The prevailing trend is now integrated teamwork supporting business strategy. When applied to Sales and Marketing it becomes Smarketing.

Smarketing = An integrated Business Strategy that boosts Sales Performance by aligning Sales and Marketing with the way that modern Customers buy.

It can be applied to anything from single accounts or specific deals, to transforming the entire Revenue Funnel.

As I will elaborate later, in either case, the likely outcome will be higher win rates, elevated revenue and profits, more accurate forecasting, happier employees and more satisfied clients.

Who would not want that for their business?

Organizations that ignore this opportunity will hand their nimbler and more innovative competitors an unfair advantage.

In today's marketplace, effective Smarketing can make the difference between huge success and dismal failure.

The degree to which your organization collaborates today is a leading indicator of how well, or how poorly, your organization is equipped to cope with change and, by association, how resilient it is.

Our own research, as well as that of many highly regarded research bodies, shows that those organizations that deploy the most up-to-date collaboration methods and tools are those that will best be able to translate their collective efforts into short- and long-term business and financial success.

Chapter Takeaway

Smarketing establishes a consistent and bi-directional feedback loop between your Sales and Marketing people that breaks down internal barriers to sales revenue and profit growth.

Crucially, Smarketing is not a shortcut, not a quick fix 'Band-Aid' solution that may fall apart after a short while. It is a holistic and sustainable solution to grow sales results, one that can be deployed quickly anywhere in the world and with little disruption to your business.

It can be deployed on individual deal pursuits or holistically to the entire revenue supply chain.

Peter Strohkorb

Chapter 3:
Time to Go Smarketing

So far, I have described the issues that today's sales and marketing teams are facing. It is time to tell you how I came to develop Smarketing and to write this book.

It didn't happen overnight. It is the fruit of more than 15 years of personal experience working in executive sales and marketing roles for some of the largest brands on the planet.

I watched carefully, noticing which strategies worked and which ones didn't. As I began to develop a coherent theory on this inter-team collaboration, my observations were supported by academic research and findings from some of the finest specialist firms in the world. Finally, I conducted my own research, asking the questions I felt that researchers and academics had missed. The observations that I made over those years led me to this conclusion:

> **Sales and Marketing are in a collaborative crisis.**
> **Sometimes it's obvious, sometimes it flies under the radar.**

I have certainly experienced first-hand the frustrations that can abound on both sides when Sales and Marketing do not cooperate effectively. I have seen good Marketing people spend valuable time, effort and money producing content and leads for the sales team, only to see them not being followed up.

Across on the other side, I have personally heard salespeople say that Marketing is useless, is not supporting them and that Sales would be better off creating its own marketing. Can you imagine the consequences that this could entail in terms of lost selling time on the one hand, and loss of brand cache on the other?

I have personally experienced the many failures and frustrations that result from unnecessarily wasted time, effort, and money on both sides.

The crux of the challenge is that the longer this disconnect continues, the further apart it drives each side from the other.

They often retreat deeper and deeper into their respective silos, behaving like jilted lovers, eventually shutting each other out completely. Hurtful finger-pointing and blame-shifting often follows.

And just like it is with jilted lovers, the disconnect often becomes personal.

Over the years, I have witnessed some downright nasty comments being lobbed back and forth.

To illustrate this, here are some lowlights:

A mid-ranking sales manager at a global technology vendor, pulling a face like he had just bitten into a lemon, had this to say about the marketing team in his organization: "What would they know about selling? Real men carry sales targets." The implication – not difficult to detect – is that Marketing is just full of sissies with scant understanding of the "real world" that sales reps inhabit. He went on to suggest that marketers hide their shortcomings behind jargon and that they are concealing their arrogance behind talk about segmentation, targeting and positioning. You can just imagine the scene, can't you?

At the same time, marketers are no more charitable than salespeople when they speak about sales reps. One senior marketing leader in a large business advisory firm had this to say about her own organization's sales force:

"What is the difference between a sales rep and a marketer?" She paused for effect, then answered her own question: "An education!"

Ouch! Talk about a cheap shot.

The quality of her delivery suggested that she'd used this nugget before. She seemed surprised when I didn't laugh, probably because she was used to delivering the joke to her marketing peers, many of whom might share her thinly veiled belief that sales reps are all uneducated knuckle-draggers who don't have the capacity to appreciate the sophistication of all the things that Marketing does for them.

This marketing lady portrayed an unfortunately widespread feeling of superiority that salespeople so often complain about. This sentiment is based on her viewing her formally recognized academic marketing credentials over practical hands-on selling experience. Because the lady in question had gone to university, gained a tertiary qualification and was now formally recognized she felt that she had earned the right to feel superior to undergraduate salespeople.

The more I encountered these kinds of inter-departmental hostilities, the clearer it became that something had to be done to improve this situation. Luckily, there is good news on this front: I am fortunate enough to have found a sympathetic ear in ivied halls: The head of the Executive MBA program at a respected Australian university saw the light. I am proud to say that the institution and I started working together to include the notion of selling in their Executive MBA curriculum. We are now even talking about a graduate or maybe post-graduate qualification in Sales Management as a stand-alone subject. Given the antipathy with which most marketing lecturers view Sales this is revolutionary stuff!

My sincere hope is that the tertiary education sector will, in time, lead to similar levels of formal qualification for sales reps and sales managers as for marketers. I understand that some countries, e.g. the USA, are well advanced on that issue.

But there is much more to this challenge than education alone. There is also a cultural issue at play.

Have you noticed the almost ingrained lack of motivation for salespeople and marketers to work together? If only I could find a way to make them want to work together, to show them, for instance, how they could increase their own productivity (as well as the revenue performance of the entire organization) through inter-departmental cooperation, then the path to Smarketing would be lit up like an airport runway at night.

The fact that the term **Sales, Marketing and Customer Alignment** has become something of a buzzword in recent years that makes it clear that organizations are starting to recognize that misalignment is a serious issue.

An issue that is worth resolving.

To me though, what is missing in all the talk is the subject of the human element. After all, people are the unifying glue that bridge the chasm.

Surely, there can be no guarantee of success unless the people involved are motivated at a personal level to work together, preferably towards a common goal.

I will say it again in a slightly different way: You can have the most sophisticated processes and the latest technology, but if your people are not working together, all your efforts will come to nothing.

The moment I recognized this, a passion was kindled in me to identify the right balance of these elements that could finally close the gap between Sales and Marketing. With this passion as my starting point, I developed, tested, and refined my solution. I called it Smarketing.

To the best of my knowledge, I am the first to offer a dedicated method to bring together both functions across the sales and marketing divide to recognize and understand the critically supportive roles that their each play, how they can make best use of their respective skill sets and competencies and teach them how they can come together as one team to the benefit of the entire organization.

We need to get away from that silo mindset, where Sales and Marketing operate largely independently with few shared processes, KPIs, or metrics.

That is not Smarketing.

Collaboration happens between people. It makes jobs more enjoyable, it gives that spice that makes people want to come to work, to do great things together, to achieve and to succeed.

People are, after all, not robots. We are human, and humans are more complicated than lifeless processes and metrics. We are ambitious, proud, and emotional. We crave personal recognition, fulfillment, and satisfaction, we fear failure and ridicule. Processes and technologies simply cannot account for these feelings. We need to go deeper to a more fundamental place: To the human heart at the center of the challenge, to a place where Smarketing lives.

Chapter Takeaway

Throughout this book and in this chapter, I make a somewhat impassioned plea in favor of collaboration. It is this same passion that inspires my writing, my speaking, my coaching, and my consulting work. It led me to develop Smarketing and to help organizations to improve their performance.

Chapter 4:
The Many Business Benefits of Smarketing

My vision for Smarketing is to create a world in which organizations reach and consistently remain at a high level of performance because their Sales and Marketing people work harmoniously together as one team. Admittedly, that can be viewed as pretty vague in the eyes of fact-driven Executives.

Very few CEOs that I know will approve funding for a new strategic initiative without at least a basic appreciation of the expected business, people and financial returns, and of the anticipated time to benefits realization.

So, what can organizations expect from Smarketing?

To start off with, here are statistics from some of the most authoritative companies around:

LinkedIn

No lesser authority than LinkedIn says in its 2020 report, called "Sales and Marketing, The Odd Couple" that:

- ✓ "85% of sales and marketing leaders say sales and marketing alignment is the largest opportunity for improving business performance today"
- ✓ "87% of sales and marketing leaders say collaboration between sales and marketing enables critical business growth"
- ✓ "90% of sales and marketing professionals agree that when initiatives and messages are aligned, the customer experience is positively impacted"
- ✓ "98% of sellers and 97% of marketers think that bad alignment negatively impacts the business and the customer"

https://business.linkedin.com/content/dam/me/business/en-us/marketing-solutions/cx/2020/images/pdfs/moments-of-trust-v4.pdf

Forrester

International market advisory firm Forrester says in its 2019 report "ABM Maturity Corresponds To Better Revenue Results" that

- ✓ "Marketing and sales teams that take an ABM approach together can be up to six percent more likely to exceed their revenue goals than teams that are less ABM-advanced"
- ✓ "62 of marketers say they can measure a positive impact since adopting ABM"

https://www.forrester.com/report/Forrester+Infographic+ABM+Maturity+Corresponds+To+Better+Revenue+Results/-/E-RES157155

Altify

Altify, in is 2017 "Business Performance Benchmark Study"* quantifies the sales productivity benefits of closer collaboration between sales and marketing teams:

"18 percent shorter sales cycles and 26 percent higher win rates."
- Altify Report

* https://www.altify.com/benchmark2017/

The report goes further.
Imagine what difference the following numbers could make in your business, and also for you personally:

- ✓ Up to 4 times higher sales productivity
- ✓ Up to 227 percent more sales revenue
- ✓ Up to 36 percent more gross profit
- ✓ Up to 42 percent higher sales lead conversion rates
- ✓ Up to 33 percent faster ramp-up time for new sales reps

I have personally seen Smarketing deliver revenue growth from as little as 2.7 percent to as high as 24 percent. This is not taking into account the boosting effect that Smarketing can have on third-party tech solutions. Further, this does not include the impact of a more collaborative, positive and enjoyable work environment, one in which staff is happy, supportive and being supported. Most importantly, they're not thinking about leaving for the perceived greener pastures of perhaps more collaborative competitors. Staff turnover is reduced, and as any CFO will tell you, that factor represents a significant cost saving that goes straight to the bottom line.

Even those organizations that received relatively low financial returns (e.g. in the 2-3 percent ROI range) were happy because, while the percentages do not sound impressive by themselves, the absolute/total revenue amounts that they gained were in the millions of dollars, which was well in excess of what their Smarketing deployment had cost them. In other words, for every dollar that our clients give us to help them build a more collaborative organization, we typically give them ten dollars back in productivity gains.

While implementing Smarketing our clients also learn something new about their business and their people. This kind of in-depth understanding of your employees and the ways in which they can be encouraged to work together for the better of the whole organization may not have a hard dollar figure attached to it, but the so-called "soft benefits" should also play a part in your calculations of the ROI of Smarketing. All kinds of organizations, and the people within them, received untold benefits from Smarketing. I will provide you with real-world examples in Chapter 13.

In addition to these 3rd party statistics, here are some real-world achievable returns:

- ✓ up to 36 percent higher gross profit (as Marketing will create more of the collateral that salespeople will actually use)

- ✓ up to 23 percent higher lead conversion rates (as the right kind of collateral will finally accelerate sales velocity)

- ✓ up to 27 percent more sales revenue (because salespeople will spend more of their time selling, not creating their own marketing collateral)

- ✓ up to 33 percent faster ramp-up for new sales reps (because better collaboration attracts superior talent)
- ✓ lower technology risk (as improved collaboration helps people to understand why they should use the technology and boosts technology acceptance, utilization, and end-user compliance)
- ✓ lower organizational risk (as organizations retain, and can now leverage, the acquired skills and know-how of their top sales performers)
- ✓ improved morale (because Marketing staff will enjoy a better relationship with Sales, and vice versa)

Smarketing delivers tangible business results for all your stakeholders. Here is a summary for you:

1. **Customer Benefits**

Your organization becomes one that your customers want to do business with. They recognize you as:

- A trusted brand
- A reliable business partner
- A competent advisor
- A competitively priced vendor
- A consistently high performer
- A valuable customer experience

2. **Marketing Benefits**

Better alignment and deeper collaboration with Sales, resulting in:

- Less effort wasted on content that the sales team does not use (i.e. more effective utilization of Marketing resources)
- Greater recognition from the sales team of Marketing's contribution to results
- Better decision-making due to more complete and up-to-date information
- Less scrutiny of the Marketing budget due to improved performance and the more positive perspective of the sales team on Marketing's more actively supportive role

3. Sales Benefits

More effective support from Marketing help to better differentiate the organization from its competitors, to lift its brand, better engage with the right prospects and customers, and to achieve and exceed sales targets:

- Accelerate sales velocity
- Retain high sales margins
- Reduce discounting
- Un-stick stuck sales
- Boost the sales performance of even average sales performers

4. C-Suite Executive Benefits

A future-proof, more agile organization with:

- Accurate forecasts
- More revenue
- Higher profits
- Lower risk
- Less staff turnover
- Raised morale
- More resilient and responsive teams
- A work environment that attracts top performing-talent

The above are the stakeholder benefits.

Next, let us take a closer look at some of the organizational benefits that you can expect from Smarketing.

1. Better Communication

Smarketing solves challenges in any organization in which the communication between Sales and Marketing is less than ideal. Sales may know how to sell, and Marketing may know how to market, meaning they both know how to speak to people outside of the organization, but they might need a little guidance talking to each other in more productive ways.

Smarketing provides that structure.

Of course, in situations where it becomes clear that Sales, Marketing, or both can reap substantial benefits from further training or coaching that may be less related to best practice collaboration (such as sales training, leadership coaching or marketing consulting, for instance) my method will make these support tools so much more effective than they would otherwise be.

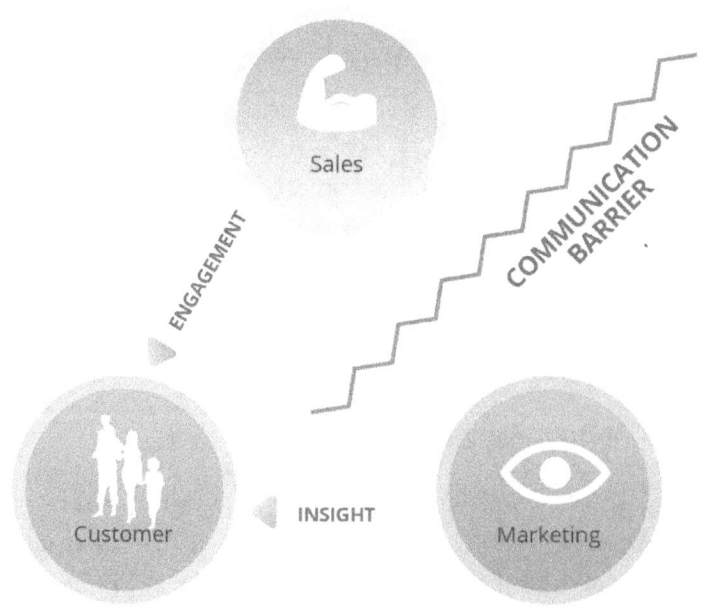

Without Smarketing:
Communication breaks down and customer experience suffers.

2. Closer Collaboration

Smarketing establishes a 360-degree continuous feedback loop between Sales and Marketing so that they can collaborate more easily and much more effectively. But it also goes further as it can now also include feedback from your customers, which is interesting if you want to know how your marketing messages and your sales efforts are being perceived by your target audience.

The 360-Degree Collaboration loop ensures that Sales can keep Marketing informed on which marketing support really works for them, and which, in turn, allows Marketing to focus on doing more of what is working for Sales and less of what isn't.

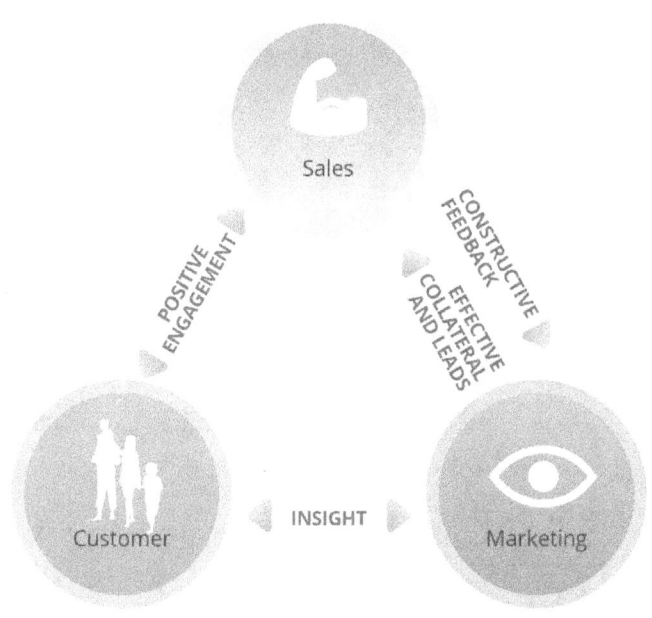

With Smarketing: It's a Win-Win-Win Situation

Each team can now focus on its own competencies yet support the other in working towards a more positive business outcome for all parties involved.

You may even choose to include some of your customers in this initiative. You see, Smarketing becomes even more powerful for those organizations that are brave enough to include some of their key customers in the feedback loop.

While some executives might fear that this arrangement may open up the organization to the airing of their dirty linen, it also brings a powerful sense of partnership to the vendor-client relationship.

It is a classic win-win-win scenario. Who would want to reject that?

3. A Highly Collaborative Business Environment

Through the power of Smarketing, you end up with an organization where the lines between Sales and Marketing blur to the point where they become almost indistinguishable.

- They are like yin and yang, i.e. Sales and Marketing people work as one team and become far more effective.
- They collaborate with each other and with their key customers.
- They achieve results, both in financial and in human terms.
- They enjoy their work more.

Sales and Marketing are One Team

4. Improved Profit Performance

As you might guess, a structured program that drives Sales and Marketing effectiveness results in a substantially more effective sales force.

I have found that the most compelling case for implementation hinges upon this point, so the rest of the points in this chapter will include calculations showing you exactly what kind of ROI those implementing the Smarketing can expect.

Key to these figures is the understanding that incremental improvement to a single function can lead to dramatic holistic improvements. For long-time readers of business literature, this will not come as a new revelation. Back in 1992, Stephen Hindman and John Sviokla from the Harvard Business School investigated sales effectiveness.

This what they found:

"A company that can increase its sales-revenue-per-person productivity by just 5 percent, can increase its profit results by 20 percent. "

In other words, Smarketing can be a four-fold profit multiplier!

The impact of this statement can easily be demonstrated in a quick sample calculation.

In the following table you can compare the top line and the bottom-line results when varying the organization's focus on specific objectives by just 5 percent.

P&L Performance Impact	Base Case P&L	Reduce Direct Selling Expenses by 5%	Increase Sales Vloume by 5%	Raise Price by 5%
Sales Revenue	$100.00	$100.00	$105.00	$105.00
Cost of Goods Sold (COGS)	$60.00	$60.00	$63.00	$60.00
Gross Profit	$40.00	$40.00	$42.00	$45.00
Fixed Costs	$13.00	$13.00	$13.00	$13.00
General Admin Costs	$11.00	$11.00	$11.00	$11.00
Direct Selling Expenses	$6.00	$5.70	$6.00	$6.00
Profit Before Tax (PBT) in $	$10.00	$10.30	$12.00	$15.00
Profit Before Tax (PBT) Increase from Base Case in $	$0.00	$0.30	$2.00	$5.00
Profit Before Tax (PBT) Increase from Base Case in %	0.0%	3.0%	20.0%	50.0%

Profit Outcomes based on Three 5% Changes in Input

In the sample, we are comparing the financial impact of reducing direct selling expenses against increasing the sales volume, and against raising the price.

At first glance it looks like raising prices may be the best option. And it probably is from a purely theoretical perspective, but in the real world its ultra-competitive climate means that raising prices it is not always realistic.

The table below highlights that even just a small change (e.g. by just 5 percent) of the right parameter can make a huge difference in sales and in the financial performance for an organization.

Watch out though, because the positive effects that I have outlined above can have an equally amplifying effect when they go into negative territory (i.e. a small discount by a lazy sales rep looking for a quick sale can have a hugely negative impact on your profitability).

Please be mindful of that fact.

5. Increased Sales Revenue

Not all salespeople are alike, so, within any organization, there are top performers and what I like to call second- and third-tier performers. Though such is not always the case, let us for simplicity's sake assume that the top-tier salespeople's performance cannot be substantially improved. There is, however, a great deal of room for improvement in the bottom groups. Here is a sample calculation based on a hypothetical organization with the following assumptions:

1. The top performing tier of salespeople brings in $20m in annual sales revenue
2. The remaining salespeople bring in $50m per year

Now let us assume that Smarketing will slightly improve the performance of the middle and bottom groups of salespeople.

We are not talking about a 20 percent or even a 30 percent leap in productivity here, let's look at a very conservative 5 percent improvement.

What would that accomplish?

In a paper published by Qvidian, called "Moving The Middle", they make the following claim:

> "A 5 percent improvement among the middle 60 percent of your sales performers can deliver an over 91 percent greater revenue impact than a five percent uplift among your top 20 percent.".

https://s3.amazonaws.com/sellingpower-webinars/2014/0605/Move-the-Middle.pdf

Across-the-board knowledge sharing – especially when this knowledge is the product of Smarketing-enabled dialogue – can substantially impact the bottom 80 percent of your sales force, enabling and empowering them with the agility and collateral they need to lift their performance considerably.

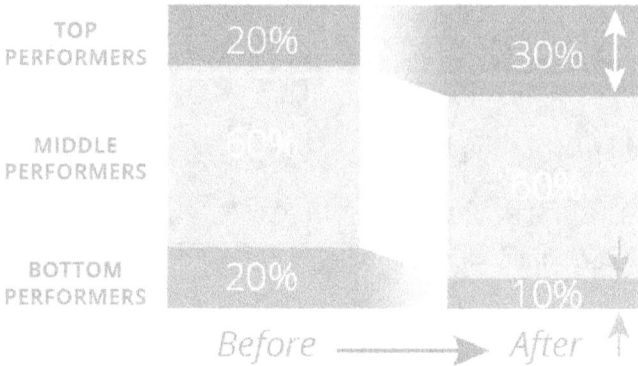

Boosting the Sales Performance of Middle and Low Performers has a greater revenue impact than boosting Top Performers alone

This means that extracting your top performers' personal sales know-how and corporate knowledge and transferring it to reps further down the chain is proven to lift the performance of lesser-performing reps and can have immense positive overall productivity benefits.

Next, is a sample calculation for a fictitious sales organization with $100m in annual revenue. For illustration purposes I have kept the sales targets and rep numbers constant in the before and after scenarios. The simple calculation shows that improving the sales performance of the middle and low performers **by just 10 percent** will yield $7 million worth of additional sales revenue per year, and, assuming a gross margin of 30 percent, the business would be rewarded with $2.1 million more profit!

(Please note the heading in the table below. The OneTEAM Method® is how we implement Smarketing into organizations.)

	Before OneTEAM Method (Baseline)	After OneTEAM Method Year 1
Annual Sales Target (assume constant)	$100,000,000	$107,000,000
# of Salespeople (assume constant)	100	100
Total Sales Team Revenue Contribution (assume constant)	$30,000,000	$30,000,000
2nd Rate Sales Team Revenue Contribution	$60,000,000	$66,000,000
Bottom Sales Team Revenue Contribution	$10,000,000	$11,000,000
Total Actual Sales	$100,000,000	$107,000,000
Revenue Increase due to sales effectiveness of the bottom and mid-level team increased by just 5%		$7,000,000
Sales Profit it at 30% margin		$21,000,000

How would you like that sort of additional revenue and profit each year for your business?

6. Fewer Lost and "No Decision" Deals

For comparison purposes, we are assuming here the same size of organization as in the example above. Additionally, we are assuming that Smarketing can improve the confidence and ability of the sales force to build more effective relationships with its Prospects to unstick **a very conservative 5 percent** of previously lost or 'no decision' sales per year.

If Smarketing can reduce the number of lost or stuck sales by just 5 percent, then in our example it will result in a revenue increase of over $3 million and $1 million in additional profit per year!

As you can see, even a small improvement in the support that the sales force receives from Marketing will have a dramatic effect on the organization's overall financial health.

7. Reduced Risk

It is an age-old wisdom that your star employees go home at the end of each workday with a wealth of know-how and corporate intel locked away in their heads.

What if they leave and go to your competitor? What would happen if your organization were to fall behind competitors that are adopting Smarketing initiatives?

A joint research venture between MathMarketing and Marketo showed that alignment between Sales and Marketing departments on sales lead generation and management resulted in 67 percent higher probability that marketing-generated leads result in new revenue

(http://www.marketo.com/reports/2013-sales-and-marketing-alignment-study/).

If these numbers are true just for this narrow band of sales lead-related interactions, can you imagine what Smarketing could achieve across the board for an organization?

In summary:

**If an organization with $100m in annual revenue can lift its sales performance by just 5 percent,
then the ensuing difference is $5 million higher revenue
and 1.5 million more gross profit!**

8. Attract and Retain Better Talent

No matter how in-demand your product or service, without a world-class staff to locate, nurture, and maintain relationships with your customers, you'll consistently fall short of greatness. True business success means the ability to attract, train and retain the best and brightest people around.

Apart from remuneration, the key to attracting and keeping top-rate talent lies in a positive culture. Ontario's OYG Inc. says that, if you want to attract and retain quality talent, the most important thing you can do is "understand your current culture".

This can hardly come as a surprise. Where would you rather work? In a bellicose culture where people go to battle with each other every day, or in a cooperative and collaborative culture, one in which staff not only help each other, they want their co-workers (even those in different departments) to succeed.

The ability to establish a culture-based reputation endows an organization with the power to attract and retain high-performing salespeople, which itself delivers real dollar benefits to an organization. Smarketing includes a series of financial models that helps our clients to identify their low hanging fruit and accordingly to priorities the method implementation.

9. Superior Customer Experiences

I have talked about the Buying Journey in which Buyers conduct their own research until they feel ready to talk to a sales rep. I also mentioned how critically important it is that the value messaging of online content matches that of the sales rep when the Buyer is ready to talk to a salesperson.

As the saying goes: "A confused mind says No."

Nothing much puts a potential Buyer off more than inconsistent value messaging.

Smarketing ensures that the messaging between online content and personal experience remains consistent and it thus addresses the risk of disconnect at this critical juncture in the Buying Journey.

The benefits that collaboration brings in its wake are many, and it can have substantial flow-on effects: a collaborative spirit infuses almost everything that a company does, and customers notice it.

Chapter Takeaway

It is probably not realistic to expect all these benefits to come through at the same time, but it is obvious that these benefits are accumulative and substantial. There are both tangible and intangible business benefits to Smarketing. The tangible benefits alone are significant, whereas the intangible benefits of job satisfaction, a supportive work environment and team collaboration make for an altogether nicer place to work. As most of us tend to spend more than a third of our working days at work, isn't that also something that is worth investing in?

Peter Strohkorb

Chapter 5:
The Top 7 Smarketing Mistakes

There is a classic saying in business:

> *The seven most dangerous words in business are:*
> *"We have always done it this way."*
> - Anonymous

In my twenty years of working in both executive sales and strategic marketing roles for some of the world's largest corporations, I have personally witnessed the degree to which waste and frustration abound when Sales and Marketing collaborate poorly.

My experience has taught me time and again that this waste of time, money, resources and lost opportunities for revenue growth are thoroughly avoidable.

Imagine an organization in which there is a symbiotic relationship between Sales and Marketing; an organization in which each department knows exactly what the other needs in order to be successful; an organization in which proactive inter-departmental communication hones content to a fine point and makes the most from sales leads; an organization that shares and responds to customer feedback and market insight on a macro level.

Such an organization, no matter what its products or services, would be either an industry leader or well on its way to becoming one. Such an organization would enjoy the envy of its peers, the trust of its clients and the support of its owners and shareholders.

At every turn, our research and my experience have led me to the same conclusion: The way to make both departments stronger is to establish – as early as possible – to focus both parties on a common and shared goal. This goal may be a set and agreed sales target, but I find it even better if the shared goal focuses not only on internal organizational results, but also on customer satisfaction and experience.

When this is effectively managed, a collaborative corporate culture also makes an organization more attractive to quality workforce candidates; it can boost staff morale and make it easier to recruit and retain high-quality talent.

Collaborative businesses are not only more successful, but they are also magnetic. They pull high-value customers and high-quality staff into their orbit and keep them there.
- Peter Strohkorb

While Smarketing can dramatically improve both sales and marketing functions in an organization, there is a right way and a wrong way to implement and facilitate true collaboration.

Knowing where the opportunities and threats are makes the job all the easier, so let's look at the places where would-be collaborators most frequently founder.

Mistake #1: Doing Nothing

The worst mistake anyone can make is to turn a blind eye to challenges and opportunities.

Denying that there is room for improvement, or merely accepting the *status quo*, can magnify issues that would be otherwise manageable.

In far too many companies, sales and marketing departments are working in their respective silos, largely unaware of, or ill-equipped for, the changing world that surrounds them. Too many organizations have taken this path and suffered for it. How did Kodak miss the digital-camera revolution? How did Canon not see the threat from smartphones with in-built cameras?

Doing nothing is a high-risk strategy.

At perhaps a more tactical level, this challenge manifests itself when sales reps using twentieth century selling techniques are unable to get their foot in the door with their twenty-first-century customers. The new Buyer expects reps to approach them well prepared and with a complete understanding of their challenges; they want added value and subject-matter expertise; they want content, not pitches. Anything less than suitable and sustainable solutions that respond to their specific needs and they will start to look towards the competition. To address this demanding customer, the rep and the organization must both recognize that the customer and their buying process is no longer what he once was.

This is a challenge that must be overcome, as sitting on our hands will get us nowhere, fast.

Mistake #2: Believing that Technology alone will deliver Results

Most organizations have already implemented CRM systems, but, according to CIO.com, **between 18 percent and 69 percent of CRM projects fail at some level.**

It is easy to see why.

Even if the technology implementation goes well, my personal experience is that sales reps don't like spending their time inputting data that reports their activities to management unless they feel that this process is somehow moving sales forward. Sales Enablement (SE) technology is different in this regard, provided it is implemented in the right way. Rather than feeling that they are giving something up (be it time or information) sales reps can see quickly whether they are receiving something in return for their efforts. Having said that, technology can make well-oiled systems run better, but it will rarely increase productivity if the processes that it is applied to are bad to begin with, e.g. data quality and the underlying processes need to be relatively airtight for technology to be effective.

My own research shows that technology can be a powerful tool that is crucial to B2B sales success, but it seems that there can be such a thing as too much technology.

62 percent of the businesses I surveyed that were using CRMs as their only sales-supporting IT system saw their revenues decline. At the other end of the spectrum, running the technology gamut, i.e. implementing three or more of the following IT solutions: CRM, SE, SFA, and MA, made things much, much worse. The most technologically advanced companies are not, it seems, necessarily the most profitable ones.

As a customer-facing tool, technology extends and amplifies reach and message, but beyond a certain tipping point, it can set the customer's teeth on edge.

A wealth of customer research shows that, while automation may be effective in terms of providing sales leads, the qualification process, when automated, can alienate more Prospects than qualify them.

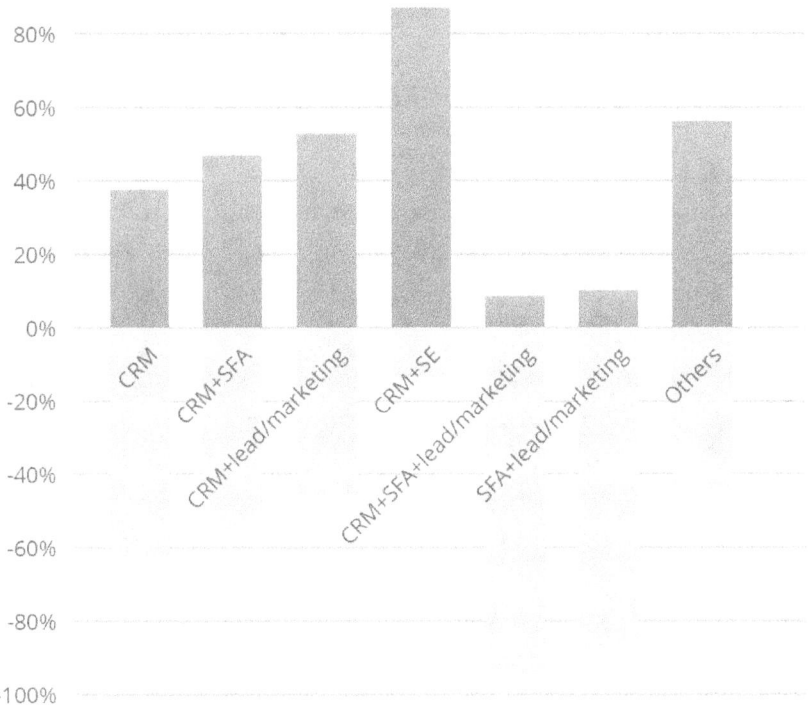

Growth Organizations   Non-Growth Organizations

Buyers who are early, or midway, through their buying process do not want to be qualified as a lead. Instead, they want to engage and discuss their challenges and how you can help solve them. Still, many Buyers of automation software are expecting this software to nurture their leads for them. To me, this kind of use of automating is not right. Automation should facilitate but never replace meaningful contact between customers and vendors.

While the number of organizations investing in CRMs continues to rise, those who have been using the technology for some time may have discovered that there is a saturation point of sorts.

This is largely due to the mistaken focus on the capabilities of the technology's, instead of the requirements of the people who use it.

It is obvious that even the most sophisticated business process technology will remain ineffective if you do not have your people aligned and engaged with that process first.

Just because software *can* do something does not mean that it will. In other words, you don't need to use all the features and functions that software offers, just the ones that actually generate a business benefit and the ones that the organization can cope with from a change management perspective.

Organizations that try to implement too much technology can very easily end up with very little business.

The core challenge is not with the under-utilized technology, it is with the sales force's resistance to supporting automation. When I have broached the topic of CRMs with salespeople, their complaints about the technology have been consistent: CRMs are, they feel, more a sales management and surveillance tool, than a sales-support instrument.

Salespeople are reluctant to give up their autonomy without anything in exchange, and that is precisely what they *are* being asked to do. What they feel is their personal IP – Prospect/customer contacts, relationships, and interactions – is being scrutinized in ever-increasing ways, and they feel like they're being hit with a double whammy: they're handing over highly valuable knowledge and they're being micro-managed more tightly.

The question that keeps on coming up in my interviews with salespeople is "What's in it for me?"

If you cannot answer that question, you'll want to take a closer look at the Productivity Trinity, which we'll discuss in detail in Chapter 11.

Mistake #3: Implementing Quick Fixes and 'Band-Aid' Solutions

The world is increasingly impatient, and so are we; our attention spans are getting shorter, so it is no wonder that, when challenges arise, we look for quick fixes. Shortcuts and roundabouts rarely work when it comes to Smarketing. When reps do not make their targets, many organizations try to address the challenge with one or all of the following three short-term, 'quick fix' solutions.

Popular Quick Fix: Hiring More Reps

The rationale for this popular choice is as follows: if **X** number of reps brings in **Y** amount of revenue, then increasing **X** will increase **Y** as well.

However, hiring new sales reps is not a step that one should take lightly. There is considerable risk and cost associated with the hiring process.

According to Brainshark, the average cost of onboarding new sales staff can be as high as US$100,000 per employee, and an average of 11.2 man-months is spent on hiring, onboarding and training. That is the cost before the rep even puts his or her feet under their desk!

https://www.brainshark.com/ideas-blog/2018/october/sales-onboarding-stats

Simply adding more staff is rarely the solution to poor sales performance. On the contrary, adding new staff without addressing the underlying issues that are at the heart of poor sales performance is the equivalent trying to break up a brawl between cats and dogs merely by adding one more dog to the mix.

Popular Quick Fix: Providing More Sales Training

This is a very popular quick fix, but it is also lazy and ineffective for the reasons I will outline below.

Yes, it has the advantage of ticking the 'completed' box for many sales managers who carry sales training or up-skilling as part of their KPIs. Most sales managers rarely attend or even participate in this sales training, though. Instead, they send their reps on a two- or three-day sales training course and, as if through magic, expect them to come back enlightened, motivated, and cooperative. Managers might expect their reps to be as enthusiastic about the training as they are, but since the reps' sales targets are rarely adjusted to compensate for the lost selling time, they may feel as though training is more hindrance than help. For those who are really struggling to meet their targets, training courses can feel like an outright punishment.

According to the nineteenth-century German psychologist Hermann Ebbinghaus, 87 percent of new knowledge is forgotten within 30 days (http://en.wikipedia.org/wiki/Hermann_Ebbinghaus).

What do you think happens after 30 days after the sales training?

Most of this training comes with little to no post-training follow up. The sales training often ends with a meek "send us an email if you have any more questions," which is hardly useful when the sales rep is standing in front of a customer or on a deadline to finish a sales proposal.

Perhaps I'm being a little uncharitable to sales trainers when I say that I am not aware one of very many formal sales training programs that insist on making the ongoing coaching of individual reps compulsory, after the initial sales training days are finished. In my opinion, it is neither fair nor realistic to expect anyone to execute a new method immediately (let alone successfully) after the learning experience without some degree of follow-up that nurtures them up their personal learning curves. 'Set and forget' does not work in sales training.

Another Popular Quick Fix: Generating More Sales Leads

More leads is another sure-fire way to boost sales results, right? Well, it would be if all your sales lead creation and management processes were perfect, i.e. if Sales and Marketing were working harmoniously together to generate, nurture, hand over, advance, close and report on leads perfectly. If that evaluation is not in place, why would you want to spend good money creating more leads, only to see them go nowhere?

Increasing MQL volume only has a positive effect when Sales is suffering from a lack of leads and if the leads are of acceptable quality. If it is the low quality of the leads that is driving poor sales numbers, then stuffing more leads into a flawed sales funnel will not likely achieve the hoped-for results.

"More" does not automatically equal "better".

Let us now move on to the next Sales and Marketing collaboration mistake.

Mistake #4: Having no dedicated Person or Team responsible for Smarketing

Sales and Marketing obviously both need to work together and focus on the Customer, not on what they're selling.

For such cooperation to be possible, cross-functional processes need to be in place to make sure that both sides are in alignment with their Customer.

So, who is responsible for reaching across the aisle? Is it up to Marketing to work together with Sales, or is it vice versa? What happens when they can't come together on their own initiative?

The best way to achieve success is to have a dedicated but neutral third party in place whose job it is to ensure that the collaboration between Sales and Marketing is implemented and maintained. They can get the dialogue started so that both sides can agree on what processes and metrics will be applied moving forward. This mediated dialogue can often defuse any burgeoning issues before they escalate. Before any kind of cooperation can begin, it is important that all parties agree on the process steps, the definitions and the underlying metrics, otherwise communication issues – latent or blatant ones – will merely exacerbate the situation.

Get a referee on board.

Mistake #5: Neglecting the Human Element

When attempting to foster a cooperative relationship between Sales and Marketing, it is important to address the human dimension immediately. Few things are as powerful as the realization that, often, everybody within an organization is purpose aligned – we are all pulling at the same rope, all trying to achieve the same outcome. When Sales and Marketing are at loggerheads, it is easy for both sides to forget this. Sales and Marketing need to understand and agree on *what* their roles are and how those roles relate to other roles within the organization. Only then will it be appropriate to move on to *how* each department can support the other; only then can we move on to the nuts and bolts of setting up joint processes and shared metrics.

Your marketing messaging and your sales messaging really should be aligned so they speak with a single voice and do not risk confusing the Buyer, particularly at the sensitive juncture in the Buying Journey when the Buyer moves from online research to contacting a human sales rep. Having just returned from a sales conference in the USA, I can tell you that everybody there offered only point solutions on that theme. The messages have been familiar for some time now: "Just use our sales training," "Just adopt our marketing messaging system," "Just get our leadership coaching program," and of course "Just deploy our app or install our software". The reason that I call them Point Solutions is that they resolve only a small symptom without addressing the underlying causes.

To me, this is like not seeing the forest for the trees. Since nobody is pulling all the collaboration aspects together, success is short-lived at best and elusive at worst. Though there was plenty of discussion focused on sales lead process management – especially when technology could be deployed – but there was no mention at the conference of **people** working together.

This is what makes Smarketing different, and this is what makes it so powerful.

Collaboration can be a deeply inter-personal matter. This is why Smarketing starts with the *people* dimension. Only once the people within an organization are ready, and willing, to collaborate will technology solutions land on truly fertile ground. Not apps, but people need to come first.

Mistake #6: Trying to implement Change without Executive Buy-In

When change touches on aspects of corporate culture, implementing reforms can be an uphill battle.

As laudable as it might be for middle managers or even junior staff to attempt cultural change, such optimistic projects are often doomed to fail. Unless, that is, they have executive buy-in.

This does not mean that change must come solely from the top. However, there does need to be a chorus of nodding heads all the way up there.

Remember, senior executives are time-poor; they like low risk and fact-driven initiatives. The key to getting senior executives on board is to present them with a compelling business case that is rich with data to back up the arguments.

In other words: Have a plan, and get the boss involved to support it.

"You all get along now, OK?"

When you do get the boss involved make sure there is an agreed and structured plan in place to deliver your Smarketing transformation. Platitudes will get short shrift from executives.

Mistake #7: Expecting immediate Results

Too often, we expect overnight results, and sometimes even that's not fast enough. The fact is that any change must be given time to work its way through the system if it is to have any chance to produce positive outcomes. There very well may be a quick win that can be realized in the short term, but the bigger wins almost always take time. Don't expect or demand anything to happen overnight. Technology implementation, like metric or process adjustments, can take longer than you think to have a tangible, bottom-line impact.

As we have all learned at some point or another, patience pays dividends. Smarketing, when done right, is not as simple as plugging in a new device or as flicking a switch. It will produce the kind of results that will make the investment more than worthwhile.

Chapter Takeaway

The above list is not exhaustive, but the items are surprisingly widespread in many organizations that I encounter.

It strikes me that avoiding them would be a relatively simple matter if would-be collaborators knew what to look for, what to expect, and what to avoid. Even before that, though, must come the penny-dropping realization that something is amiss and that something must be done to address the challenge. That is why I put 'Doing Nothing' at the top of my list of mistakes here.

Chapter 6:
Measuring Smarketing Maturity

The digital economy and the Buying Journey have revolutionized the way that people and organizations buy, particularly when it comes to complex B2B sales.

While it was once enough to have a relationship with one's customers to secure their loyalty, it has become increasingly apparent that, especially in competition-saturated vertical markets, the quality of these relationships is a driving factor in attracting, satisfying and retaining more customers.

Sales and Marketing are among the most customer-facing functions in any organization. These two functions may not be represented in boardrooms, but they certainly are the organization's face in the marketplace. Customers gauge you by the way your sales and marketing departments speak to them.

Since today's Buyers report that they are looking for quality, value and a consistently excellent customer experience from their suppliers, you would think that any vendor's senior management team's top priority would be to ensure that these two vital functions perform in perfect harmony so that they best represent the organization to customers and prospects.

Smarketing is the ideal vehicle to align customer-facing business processes and value messaging in order to enhance the customer experience all along the Buying Journey.

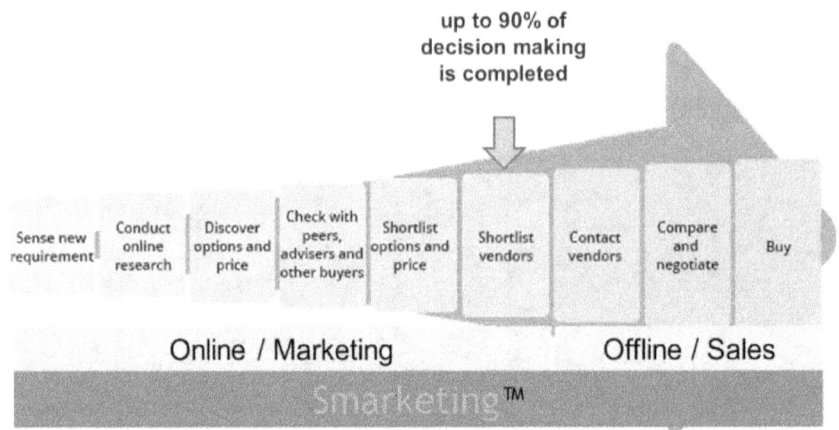

The Buying Journey

In fact, given the aforementioned customer expectations, Smarketing can be your strategic advantage.

Therefore, symbiotic Smarketing needs to become more than "a nice to have". It needs to become a top priority.

If your organization is not either overhauling or fine-tuning this important relationship right now, you can be sure that your business is at risk of falling behind.

Peter Drucker famously said that you can't manage what you can't measure.

So, how do you measure the collaboration quality between your sales and marketing teams?

I posit that there is a "Smarketing Maturity Spectrum", i.e. measurably distinct levels of Smarketing effectiveness. On the next few pages I will outline this concept in more detail and prescribe the three Smarketing Maturity levels in any organization.

The Silo Mindset

The lowest maturity level is characterized by what I call "The Silo Mindset".

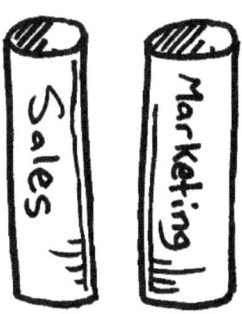

Here, the two corporate departments co-exist, often without much interaction but with lots of prejudice. This is the typical scenario where Marketing throws sales leads and collateral "over the fence" to Sales and subsequently wipes its hands of any downstream outcomes. "We've done our job." they say, "Now it's up to Sales to do theirs."

Sales looks at these leads and says, "They are no good." and just ignores them. The same process is repeated with marketing collateral.

Sales hastily concludes that Marketing doesn't support the sales effort, nor understand what Sales needs.

Marketing, on the other hand, jumps to its own conclusions, often ridiculing the sales team's selling capabilities.

This kind of vicious cycle will not, in my experience, be resolved by itself. It needs help, often external help, to overcome.

The Process Mindset

The next maturity level is what I call "The Process Mindset". At this point, the two departments have realized that they are better off working together in some limited way.

Process Mindset collaboration is limited to a small number of processes, often narrowly defined. The most popular of these seems to be the generation, nurturing and handover of sales leads. This is also one of the popular 'quick-fix solutions' that management likes to throw at the challenge of poor Smarketing.

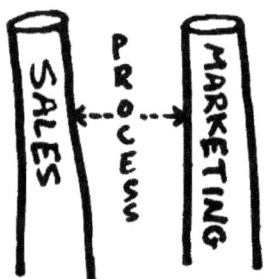

Less mature organizations treat sales lead management as a one-way process as I described above, whereas in the more mature organizations this process is bi-directional, with information flowing back and forth between Marketing and Sales in terms of lead follow up and closure rates, giving Marketing the opportunity to make adjustments towards more positive outcomes.

But even this arrangement is less than ideal.

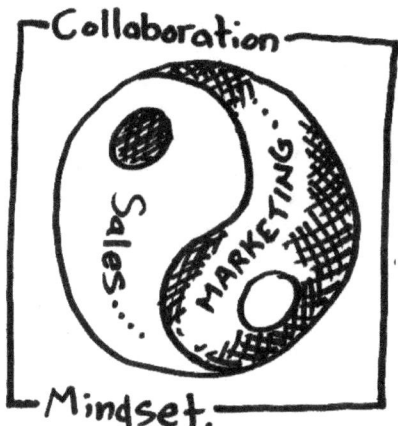

Mature organizations have discovered that there is much more to marketing than running events, the generation of sales leads and the creation of brochures and other marketing content.

These mature organizations understand the importance of a united front, i.e. from the customer's perspective, Sales and Marketing have become nearly indistinguishable from each other.

They have evolved into what I call "The Collaboration Mindset", i.e. they live and breathe Smarketing.

Think of Sales and Marketing as the two legs of a long-distance runner. Since misalignment between sales and marketing functions and their Customer significantly impedes organizational foot speed, it is crucial that organizations not be allowed to fall into this trap.

More than ever, they need to have operational footspeed in unison for maximum efficiency. They need to use their energy to propel the organizational body so that it can nimbly out-sprint their competitors.

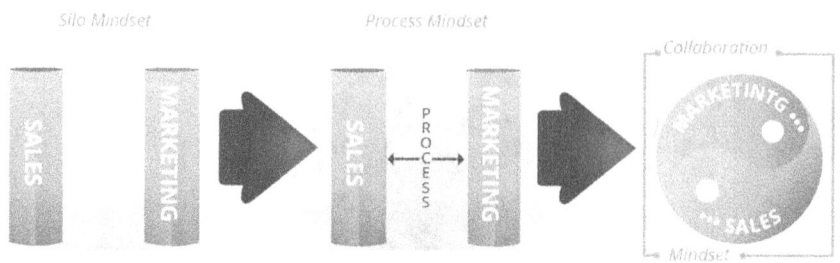

The Three Smarketing Mindsets

If you are now curious where your organization sits in terms of the above, I am happy to inform you that I have developed a sophisticated test to measure an organization's Smarketing Maturity.

It's called "The Smarketing Maturity Score" and it is further described in Chapter 12.

Or, you can take a look now at <u>peterstrohkorb.com/smarketing-test</u>

Chapter Takeaway

We looked at the three different maturity levels across the Smarketing Maturity Spectrum and the significance of knowing which stage your organization is currently in.

Please seriously consider running my Smarketing Maturity Test across your Sales and Marketing teams. The results are often a revelation.

Chapter 7:
Symptoms That Say You Need Smarketing

In this chapter we will take a detailed look at some of the symptoms that occur when you don not yet have Smarketing in your organization. Some are obvious, others perhaps less so.

So, let's investigate what they are, their potential causes, and propose some solutions.

Here are the symptoms, in no particular order:

Symptom: The Sales Pipeline is out of Control

A sales manager's reputation stands and falls with reliable sales forecasting, reporting and sales quota achievement.

Most sales organizations by now have CRM systems to make that task easier, however, there are still too many sales reps who do not use CRM systems properly.

It's human nature, really.

I mean, how many reps do you know who just love filling in forms? How many of them do you think view CRM systems as a sales management tool, rather than as a sales support tool?

Combine that with today's high expectations on sales performance and quota attainment and it becomes easy to understand why sales forecasts can become a bit "rubbery". No wonder then that many sales opportunities are being carried over and sales cycles drag on forever.

According to CSO Insights, "CRM tool adoption rates are less than 50 percent" and "Fewer than 15 percent of organizations achieved improved win rates from implementing sales tools."

Of course, the way that new apps are brought into an organization, i.e. good change management, is the key. I have been part of enough CRM and other technology implementations to notice a common mistake.

At one large multinational technology corporation that I worked with, the EVP of Sales and Marketing got up in front of the assembled crowd at the annual sales kick-off event and said these words in regard to the impending "go live" of the new combined CRM and ERP system: "We have planned everything to the nth degree. Nothing can go wrong."

If you think this sounds like the proverbial "famous last words", you can probably guess what happened next. It was, from start to finish, an unmitigated disaster. So bad was it that the vendor, the implementation consulting firm and client ended up in court, each pointing the finger at the other.

Several factors led to the high-profile failure of the project and to the ensuing sacking of the overconfident EVP. Here are some of the important lessons that the organization had to learn from this unfortunate experience:

- Do not expect staff to work on the project while also expecting them to keep performing their full-time day jobs

- Do not plan to turn off your legacy (current) system until the new system is working reliably, i.e. allow both the new and the old system to operate in parallel for a while just to make sure everything is alright before relying solely on the new system

- Do not rely on IT vendors and system integrators to act proactively in the best interest of their client, or that of the end users

- The business relationship has hit a low point when the parties feel they need to refer to the terms of their supply contract and get their lawyers involved

- Do not trivialize the users, believing that all they need is "End User Training". If you expect them to use the new system then engage them proactively right from the beginning so that they feel they are part of the journey, not just an appendix.

Why am I making this last point?

Because what happened was that all those people that had been happily using the old system and were very used to it were not really consulted when the new system was chosen and designed. They were merely expected to receive their end user training and start being productive on the new system almost instantly. Remember, in order to save cost and duplication of effort, the old system was to be shut off at the same time as the new one went live. You can guess what happened next, can't you?

Despite their end user training, the back-end staff were expecting the new system to work similarly to the old one. After all, they had been expected to continue in their day job as well as absorb the intricacies of the new system. Most had taken an attitude of "I don't have time to learn the new system, I'll work it out when it goes live."

When it did, as you would expect, pretty much all the individual tasks ended up taking much longer than anyone expected, yet the tasks were expected to be completed just as quickly (if not faster) than with the old system. After all, the new system was meant to be more efficient than the old. The pressure mounted for the back-end staff and for the management team, in the end the end users rebelled.

Let's just leave it here saying that the project ended up costing twice as much and taking about four times as long as was budgeted.

This incident does not seem to be an isolated one:

In its paper, "[Connecting the Dots on Sales Performance](#)": Accenture reported the following:

"The unvarnished truth is that a technology-centric approach has consistently failed to achieve results."

* https://www.yumpu.com/en/document/read/26682185/accenture-connecting-dots-sales-performance

Just like the Band-Aid solutions that I mentioned previously, blinkered focus on a particular challenge often produces unsatisfactory and at times un-anticipated results. Automation can actually have negative revenue effects if the users are not educated in, and open to, the cooperative strategies that the technology enables. The same goes for processes which are supported by the technology but remain practically useless unless employees commit to breaking bad habits and forming new and more productive ones.

In my experience, a shared, "people-first" approach with mutually agreed objectives, processes and metrics will result in significantly higher technology adoption rates. People that participate in choosing and implementing the solution will be motivated to see the solution succeed.

Symptom: Too many Reps are not achieving their Sales Quota

This may sound like an overly broad, and perhaps even obvious, statement but it is nevertheless true that the goal of nearly every business is to grow year-on-year revenue. This expectation exerts constant pressure on the sales force. This pressure often builds to intolerable levels in organizations with poor Smarketing. The situation comes to a head when forecasts are not met and growth stalls.

It is no surprise that executives often cite disappointing sales results when they bring me into their organization. Common sense indicates that it is highly risky to wait until issues are deeply entrenched before seeking help. So, early intervention – or, even better, proactive prevention – is the key to success.

This demands no small amount of big-picture thinking. It is often hard to see the bigger picture when you are part of it. Particularly when short-term pressures such as end of month or end of quarter sales quota seem to take priority.

Therefore, it pays to have an independent set of eyes take a fresh and unencumbered look at the sales funnel. This objectivity is crucial if you want to remediate sales revenue challenges quickly and effectively.

Symptom: The Reps and the Marketing team talk more ABOUT each other, than TO each other

Inter-departmental finger-pointing and antagonisms are where poor Smarketing often comes to a head. Not surprisingly, this friction is most commonplace in organizations in which Sales and Marketing operate in their own discrete silos.

When times are good, Sales may well puff up its chest, claiming that their skills and technique make all the difference, while Marketing may say that behind strong organizational performance is its brand building, market positioning, promotional campaigns, and high-quality sales collateral, leads and content.

However, when revenue begins to fall out of alignment with sales quotas and the pressure cooker of expectations begins to be felt in both departments then inter-departmental antagonism can quickly go from latent to blatant.

Sales may start to complain about Marketing's poor-quality collateral. Marketing may counter-punch, alleging that the sales team is ineffective or even incompetent. The ensuing "us vs. them" mentality may then color the interactions between the sales and marketing departments, and the workplace can become one characterized by rivalry and mistrust.

In my experience, it is at this point that short-term solutions such as team-building exercises and offsite retreats start being floated as possible remedies. However, since these solutions rarely address the underlying issue, the desired outcomes are often short lived.

Miscommunication and mistrust can significantly impact an organization's reputation. Since Sales and Marketing are two of any organization's main customer-facing functions, poorly aligned Sales and Marketing can translate to unacceptable levels of reputational and brand risk to an organization if it is not consistently on message in all its customer interactions.

In the digital age, a poor reputation can become viral in no time and cause untold damage to an organization.

Symptom: Reps are spending too much time on non-selling activities

How much marketing-generated collateral is your sales force really utilizing? Often it comes as a surprise to find that it is less than you might think. Some organizations seem to tolerate an unacceptably large amount of marketing collateral and sales leads going to waste.

IDC is attributed as saying this:

"Only 25 percent of sales leads and marketing collateral that Marketing creates is ever used by sales teams."

"Only 25% of sales leads and collateral that Marketing creates is ever used by sales teams". IDC

Organizations are, figuratively speaking, flushing a good part of their marketing budget down the drain. This challenge is exacerbated when sales reps spend their precious selling time on producing their own, often inconsistent, marketing collateral instead.

Why would sales reps do this?

Marketing, with its strategic objective of brand and thought leadership, creates content and leads that it honestly believes are exactly what is required to support sales.

Yet, Sales often is looking for quicker and often more specific collateral to help them meet their immediate prospects' needs and their own short-term sales targets.

Smarketing: Sell Smarter, Not Harder

Eventually, sales reps feel they can no longer wait for, nor rely on, support from Marketing. Their lack of faith in Marketing leads them to take matters into their own hands. After all, they often tend to believe that they have the more immediate contact with the market and that they know what it really takes to solicit interest and gain traction with prospects.

By trying to be all things to all people, though, salespeople tend to stretch themselves thin. What is worse, in some extreme cases, they may even make statements and claims that their marketing counterparts would not stand behind.

It is baffling that marketing teams should spend good time, effort and resources creating sales collateral without knowing exactly how (or, indeed, whether) salespeople use this material.

It is equally baffling why sales professionals feel the need to go into client meetings with their own self-made collateral. Yet, this is precisely what I am encountering in the field, particularly in large organizations that have segregated Marketing and Sales teams into separate areas, e.g. on different floors, in different buildings, in different states, or even in different countries (as is so often the case in multinational firms).

In many poorly aligned organizations, Marketing creates collateral and, figuratively speaking, "throws it over the fence" to Sales, wipes its hands and declares: "That's our job done. Now it's up to Sales to sell."

Thanks to modern technology and the temptation that it can offer to forego face-to-face interactions, this entire exchange often takes place remotely, in the digital domain.

Speaking of digital domains, most organizations have a centralized network drive or a cloud-based shared file folder that is accessible by sales as well as marketing teams.

In many organizations that I have been involved with, these shared file folders are referred to as "black holes". I.e. everything that goes in is never to be seen again. Frequently, multiple versions of the same document exist across a maelstrom of files, often illogically sorted, and frequently modified until they are utterly unintelligible, unmanaged and unmanageable.

In short, they are of use to nobody.

Since salespeople often need to access on-point material in a hurry, it comes as no surprise that, as time passes, these black holes are used less and less by salespeople. Neglect begets yet more neglect, and these shared folders become little more than impenetrable time capsules, containing nothing in any way relevant to ongoing business.

Whether they communicate face-to-face or digitally, Sales and Marketing need a new set of collaboration mechanisms that allow both departments to speak to each other in a mutually clear language. A language that allows for a constructive feedback loop that enables each department to support the other.

Imagine the kind of results that organizations could see if Marketing and Sales were able to turn effective communication into concerted action.

Symptom: Marketing is pandering to the high-profile Reps

Let us face it: High-performing salespeople are no shrinking violets. They have skin thick enough to cope with rejection on a regular basis without losing heart. Also, they are trained to be persuasive, so they are accustomed to getting their way. They often have concrete ideas about what will work for them, and they want it now. They don't like waiting, for Marketing to deliver the content that they believe they need.

I have seen particularly strong-willed sales reps storm into the marketing manager's office to tell them, in no uncertain terms, what they think of their marketing-generated sales leads and collateral. They are not reluctant when it comes to offering their own opinions, and they are not shy about applying their often-considerable persuasive powers to gain the kind of material they say they need to sell more.

Marketing can find itself bending over backwards to please this extremely vocal minority, adopting collateral, and even adjusting their strategy in a misguided attempt to appease a particularly insistent set of in-house critics.

If just a handful of vocal salespeople have a monopoly over what shape marketing collateral takes, marketing messages can become confused, costly market research can go under-utilized and both departments can end up falling significantly short of what is expected of them.

Nip this in the bud by putting strategies in place to ensure that communication is a dialogue, not a monologue and that it follows Smarketing principles.

Symptom: High-performing Salespeople are leaving

A staff turnover rate that is above the industry average is never a good sign. This becomes even more critical when an organization's top talent chooses to seek supposedly greener pastures.

A high staff turnover rate, especially when this involves an organization's top performers, can pull even large organizations into a downward spiral. A company that cannot retain its most talented people is rarely able to lure other top performers into the fold.

Finding, hiring and training replacements for your top performers comes with a hefty price tag, significant risk (ask any manager who ever got a new hire wrong), and delays (on average it takes 3 to 6 months for newly hired reps to ramp up to their full performance). Combining costs and delays can rapidly widen the gulf between the forecast and the actual sales revenue figures.

There are numerous factors that can contribute to high staff turnover: Poor quality managers, a toxic culture, lower than industry-standard pay, unrealistic sales targets, etc. In my conversations with some of the top salespeople and marketers, and those who manage them, I have identified a common cause: A sense by the rep of being under-supported, which can often be traced back to poor Smarketing.

The atmosphere of hostility, the entrenched attitudes and the less-than-productive practices that typify misaligned organizations are positively repellent to top performing salespeople and marketers.

An absence of Smarketing makes the decision to move on easy for top performers. It can become just too frustrating for them to stay, particularly when they are sought-after upwardly mobile high performers.

On the other hand, morale improves dramatically in a workplace that is made more supportive through collaboration, and communication: Countless studies have shown that, as an organization's morale improves, so does its bottom line and its customer satisfaction ratings.

A Smarketing environment can dramatically affect the feelings of contentment and satisfaction within the organization. Such environments nurture existing talent and attract a whole new caliber of top candidates.

Symptom: New Sales Reps are taking too long to reach high Performance

According to the Accenture report I mentioned earlier, "Connecting the Dots on Sales Performance":

> **"Almost 78 percent of newly hired sales reps take six months, or longer, to become fully proficient at selling."**

https://www.scribd.com/document/135133313/Accenture-Connecting-Dots-Sales-Performance

The authors of the same report also estimate that, during this ramp-up phase, each new rep costs the organization in excess of US$60,000 (this figure is probably much higher today), and this cost doesn't even include the time, effort and money invested during the often lengthy and exhausting recruitment process!

The faster a new rep ramps up, the sooner the organization can see a return on both their pre- and post-hire investment. The inverse is also true: the longer reps take to ramp up, the longer it will be before the organization sees any kind of return on their investment.

Multiply this effect by the number of new hires each year and it becomes utterly transparent that waiting longer than six months for reps to ramp up is not good business.

Imagine how much better off an organization would be if its new sales reps were to ramp up faster. Even speeding up the onboarding process by as little as 10 percent can make a huge financial difference to both the employer and to the employee.

How do we accelerate this time-to-productivity?

Firstly, by having an efficient hiring process that attracts and on-boards the right kind of people into the organization. Secondly, by giving the new hire all the support they need to become productive as quickly as possible. This support ranges from having all the information that the new rep needs to find their bearing quickly at their fingertips in a concise and easily accessible format. Importantly, this needs to include the corporate and what Chuck Carey, CEO of Compendian Inc, calls "tribal knowledge", i.e. the inherent know-how of how things work in an organization. Allow new reps to tap into these resources and they will ramp up faster than ever before.

Symptom: No clear understanding of how our Customers value our sales engagement

Wouldn't it be great if Marketers had clarity around all interactions with customers and prospects, i.e. their requirements, perceptions of the marketing content and selling techniques? Armed with this knowledge, marketing teams would be much better equipped to support the sales effort in full confidence that their content and leads are hitting the right mark.

Chapter Takeaway

As we have seen, there are many symptoms of poor Smarketing.

The good news is that no matter how far these symptoms have progressed, it is never too late to address these challenges and create a collaborative environment that lifts the entire organization.

I am proposing a good first step for you in the next chapter. Have a look.

Chapter 8:
Smarketing and the Sales Funnel

The term Sales Funnel is also often referred to as a sales process, a sales pipeline, a sales cycle, or as the buying journey.

Did you know that the original concept of a sales funnel dates back to 1898?

It's no wonder then that the traditional sales funnel concept is now old and tired. It simply is no longer suited to today's selling environment because it:

- It is generic

- It is inward-looking, as it focuses on the way sellers want to measure their selling process

- It is not customer friendly, in fact, it is completely disconnected from how buyers want to buy

- It creates pressure on salespeople to close deals, instead of helping buyers to make informed buying decisions

Here is an illustration of the traditional sales funnel:

The Traditional Sales Funnel, established in 1898

So, I re-imagined, re-invented and modernized the sales funnel for today's "new normal" selling environment in 2020, and beyond.

My new, modern, 21st century Sales Funnel is far more effective, as it aligns modern Buyers with how they want to buy, not how Sellers want to sell to them.

I call it The Modern, Customer-focused Sales Funnel.

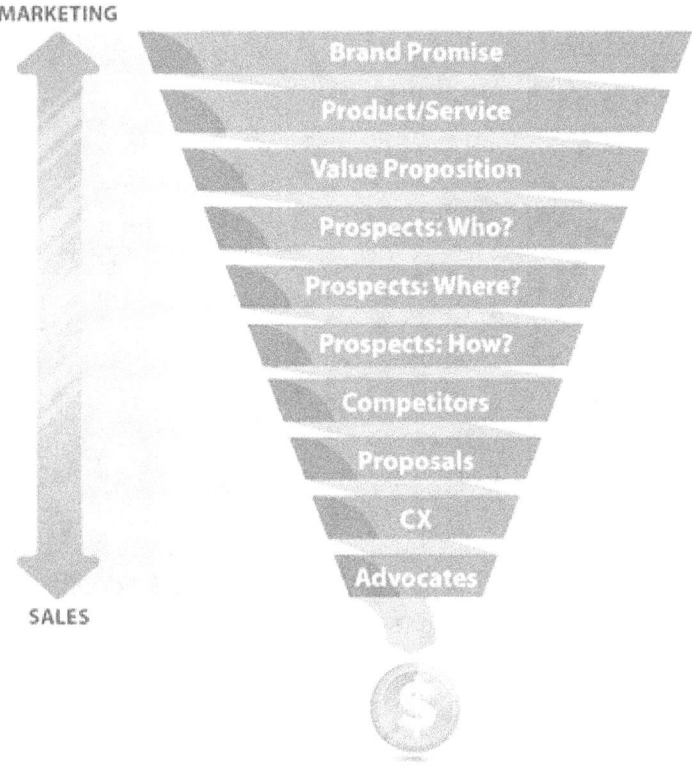

The Modern Customer-focused Sales Funnel for the 2020's

Applying modern thinking to your Sales Funnel can make a huge difference to your sales results and to your customers' experience.

Find out how much of a difference it can make in your organization in a free first advisory session with me. Book a free call with me on my website.

I recommend that you take a regular look at your funnel to check that it is still as good as it can be.

I recommend that you conduct a Sales Funnel Review at least annually as part of your sales strategy planning.

Make use of my free Sales Acceleration Assessment

Go to peterstrohkorb.com/sales-acceleration to access it.

This free assessment identifies ten (often hidden) opportunities to improve your sales funnel performance and sales velocity.

It is designed to work with any business and is also a great starting point for your own Smarketing initiative.

Hint: If you want to start right, I recommend you consider running one of my Smarketing workshops or a "The Pulse of our Business" Smarketing assessment.

It will give you your organization's Smarketing benchmarking score to kick off your Smarketing journey.

Contact me for details.

For your reference, I have pasted a summary of the ten points below.

Smarketing: Sell Smarter, Not Harder

1. A Brand that differentiates your business from your Competitors

2. A well-defined Product and/or Service to sell

3. A Unique Selling Proposition (USP) and a Killer Introduction that engages your ideal Buyers and makes them want to know more about you

4. The clear Understanding of who Your Ideal Prospects and Customers are

5. The Knowledge Where to Find them

6. The Understanding to Access and Engage Them effectively

7. The Know-how to Eliminate Your Competitors

8. The Skills to create Effective Sales Proposals that Close Deals

9. A superior pre, during and post-purchase Customer Experience

10. The Ability to keep your Customers loyal and to win their Repeat Business

Chapter Takeaway

I suggested there are ten specific opportunities to improve your sales funnel performance. They are great starting points for your Smarketing journey.

Access my 10-Point Sales Acceleration Assessment at https://peterstrohkorb.com/sales-acceleration

But be brutally honest with yourself when you are completing it.

Afterwards, contact me at pstrohkorb@peterstrohkorb.com to book a complimentary advisory session with me to explore how you can accelerate your sales, too.

Chapter 9:
The Smarketing Approach to Sales Lead Management

In 2014 my team and I conducted research into more than 100 B2B sales organizations. We separated out those organizations that had increased their revenue in the previous year, versus those that had not. We then compared their respective Smarketing Maturity with some very interesting results.

Our report shows a vast gulf that directly correlates to the way these organizations approach Smarketing, namely between those organizations that were financially successful versus the less successful ones.

> **In other words, we were able to clearly demonstrate a direct correlation between Smarketing and business success.**

A staggering 81 percent of companies that reported a decrease in sales revenue in the prior year, operate across separate sales and marketing silos.

Furthermore, growing organizations are, by and large, those that hold vastly *more* formal meetings between their sales and marketing teams, than non-growth organizations.

An astounding average of 24 percent of the less successful organizations admitted that they meet either "never", or only "annually"!

Presumably the only time the Sales and Marketing teams meet in these organizations is at their annual sales kick-off.

Perhaps unsurprisingly, more than 65 percent of companies in which sales and marketing departments reportedly meet either "never" or "annually" reported decreasing revenue.

Organizations that said they had been unable to grow their revenue over the previous 12 months also seemed to have a sizeable gap between their sales and marketing teams in terms of what they thought is most important to growing sales results.

The story was similar when we turned our focus to sales teams in successful organizations: They tended to have a more substantial overlap between their Sales and Marketing functions.

Also, the better performers in the study reported that qualifying sales leads was considered a high priority.

This is relatively obvious once you start to look at collaborative trends and how they relate to success. Less successful organizations are often those with separate performance metrics in each department. In other words, less successful organizations do not support objective alignment between the sales and marketing functions through joint metrics and KPIs.

Sales leads are a great place to start a Smarketing initiative, since they are such an obvious place of overlap for Sales and Marketing,

According to a 2019 report by CSO Insights, called "Who is Responsible for Lead Generation: Sales or Marketing?", the percentage of leads generated by sales has steadily ticked upward: 46.9 percent in

2014, 47.8 percent in 2015 and 52.6 percent in 2018. At the same time, the percentage of leads generated by marketing has dropped: 25.9 percent in 2014, 25.5 percent in 2015 and 20.2 percent in 2018.

https://www.csoinsights.com/blog/who-is-responsible-for-lead-generation-sales-or-marketing/

Incidentally, this isn't due to a lack of marketing-originated leads being fed into the sales funnel – quite the contrary.

I say that:

The issue is not with lead quantity – it is with lead quality.

[A blog post by Hubspot](#) supports this point:

> **"Unfortunately, about 61 percent of B2B marketers still send all leads they receive directly to sales,
> while only 27 percent of those leads will actually be qualified."**

https://blog.hubspot.com/marketing/lead-quality

In other words, from a salesperson's perspective, about two thirds of the leads that are being fed into the sales funnel are practically useless.

One way to make broader consensus possible is to institute solid lead scoring practices.

To put a lead-scoring system in place, though, we need to bridge a sizeable definition gap first. The evidence that this gap exists is everywhere. I have seen marketing teams that consider someone's business card a lead. Clearly this is setting the bar too low.

On the other hand, I have heard salespeople say, "I only want sales leads where the customer is ready to buy right now!" Clearly, this is setting the bar too high.

In reality, of course, the bar needs to be set somewhere between these two extremes, neither too high, nor too low – in the sales lead "Goldilocks Zone", if you like.

Technology vendors have been quick to don the superhero cape and tights, claiming they have the solution to all the issues of sales lead definitions and scoring. They have created a defined series of process steps which aim to eliminate the "No-Man's Land" in the middle of the sales funnel, as is illustrated below.

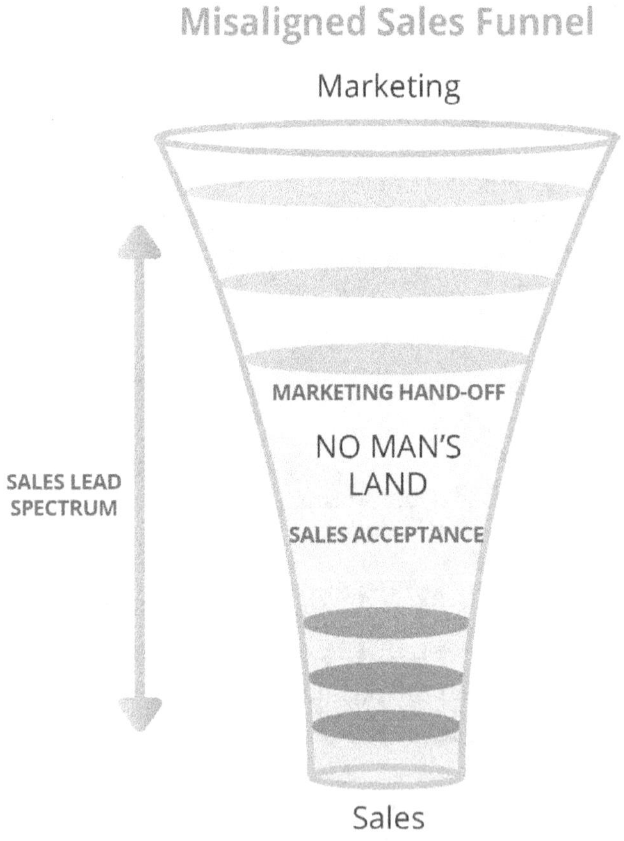

Misaligned Sales Funnel

Marketing

SALES LEAD SPECTRUM

MARKETING HAND-OFF

NO MAN'S LAND

SALES ACCEPTANCE

Sales

According to this school of thought, Marketing first generates and then nurtures the sales leads up to a mutually agreed standard.

Once that standard has been reached, Marketing hands the lead over to Sales for follow up. This gives us two new sets of definitions: Marketing-Qualified Leads (MQLs) and Sales-Accepted Leads (SALs).

While this approach is a good start, it is not the complete solution that some are claiming it to be.

For a start, they often do not value the same metrics: MQLs seem to be largely focused on the number of website interactions, clicks and downloads, whereas SALs often focus on revenue potential and time-to-deal.

I am sorry to say that I have observed that even where there is agreement on a definition for MQLs and SALs, it does not automatically produce Smarketing.

But it is possible. I have helped many organizations large and small to adjust their respective KPIs to bring their sales departments into lockstep with their marketing teams to mutual success.

Chapter Takeaway

We inspected the cooperative mindset between Sales and Marketing and looked more closely at the areas of sales lead generation and sales lead handover management.

Importantly, we discovered that alignment on MQLs and SALs does not automatically result in Smarketing, nor in positive sales revenue outcomes.

Keep this in mind for your own Smarketing implementation.

Chapter 10: Common Smarketing Implementation Roadblocks

"Errare humanum est." To err is human.

This sentence is often attributed to the Roman philosopher Seneca, who expressed that, as humans, we are not infallible.

In this chapter I will deal with some of the human perceptions and perspectives that I have encountered in my work that hinder the implementation of Smarketing.

We will begin with what salespeople have said, followed by some of the missives by marketers.

This could get interesting…

Salespeople say: "We need better leads."
It seems to me that too many internal sales processes move in one direction only, namely from Marketing to Sales. Rarely is there an opportunity for Sales to provide constructive feedback back to Marketing.

Proposed Solution:
There needs to be some accountability on the part of Marketing that the sales leads that are being fed on to Sales are indeed properly pre-qualified. Clear parameters as to what passes muster, and what does not, are important here.

This can be as simple as quick follow ups between individual team members, or it can be formalized in the CRM, or even become a formal meeting agenda to answer the question of: "How are we doing with our Smarketing?".

Salespeople say: Marketing doesn't understand how selling works.
In my opinion, Marketers do have a reasonable understanding of how selling works, but they may lack true appreciation of the pressures that salespeople are under to perform daily.

Proposed Solution:
Get Sales and Marketing on the same page through joint Smarketing meetings and workshops. Particular attention should be paid to the feedback that Sales has to offer regarding what Marketing collateral, campaigns and initiatives really work to win deals. Whenever possible, give both departments joint sign-off powers on new initiatives and have marketers shadow sales reps on their sales calls. This serves two purposes: 1. Marketers gain a better understanding of how reps operate, and 2. Sales reps gain a better understanding of how marketing people think.

Salespeople say: Marketing spends money without having much to show for it.
This is, of course, unfair to Marketing. Marketing can not be expected to advance and close sales. That is the job of salespeople. However, there are ways to bring both functions into unison.

Proposed Solution:
Though it doesn't work for all organizations, some have chosen to tie Marketing's compensation to sales revenue. In order to be at all productive, this step should only be taken as part of a more broadly implemented Smarketing strategy.

In some cases, new compensation structures have engaged Marketing to provide better qualified and nurtured leads and motivated them to more proactively support and engage with the sales process. The risk around this strategy, however, is that it may well frustrate marketers as they may feel they are being measured on outcomes they have little control over.

The Common Perceptions by Marketers

So far, we've let Sales say its piece, now it's Marketing's turn.

What is crucial to remember though is that, while many of these perceptions poorly reflect reality, none of them should be dismissed outright. In each of my proposed solutions, I suggest ways that collaborative strategies can be leveraged to deal with the roots of the challenges. Ignoring negative feedback fosters resentment. Keep that in mind as you make your way through.

Marketers say: Sales gets all the glory.
After all, a transaction is only the final stage in a long, labor-intensive, and often Marketing-originated process. It's easy to see how Marketers feel a little left out when they see all the financial incentives and rewards go to the sales team.

Proposed Solution:
Compensate Marketing for their contribution to sales results. If they are lobbing balls that Sales is knocking out of the park without breaking a sweat, there is no reason that Sales should hog all the credit and rewards.

At the same time, if Marketing is to share in the rewards, there needs to be some level of accountability to it. Compensation and revenue attribution should be related for marketers in similar ways to the way salespeople are compensated.

Engaging Marketing in the sales process can, in many cases, make a sales force significantly more productive.

I have seen empowered and motivated marketing departments spur on salespeople by allocating sales leads to those reps with the higher propensity to close them, reducing leads for those reps who are not acting on them.

As ever, collaboration works best when it is a two-way street.

Marketers say: Salespeople are incompetent.
The leads they are receiving from Marketing are well-qualified and primed, but the salespeople are unable, or unwilling, to engage with MQLs in a way that will result in a sale. They are squandering the good leads that Marketing is providing.

Proposed Solution:

This defensive response is often heard when Marketers feel they are unfairly criticized by salespeople. Of course, it is nonsense, salespeople are not incompetent. The root cause of the sentiment may lay elsewhere.

It may be worthwhile to explore which market segments are producing the highest ROI. Long sales cycles that consistently end in small purchases can look like high conversion rates but conceal poor revenue outcomes.

If your fastest sales are emerging out of markets that are being under-targeted, then re-allocating resources to focus on those markets can dramatically impact the top and the bottom line.

Marketers say: Salespeople don't understand Marketing.
This is a common complaint, but it is only partially true. Salespeople do have an appreciation of marketing, but the daily pressures to perform makes salespeople want to look for shortcuts, which is not the way that marketers operate.

Proposed Solution:
To me, this may well be a matter of mindset. What's more, it's one that frequently leads to salespeople developing their own marketing collateral and ignoring Marketing's sales leads. This unhelpful situation can be resolved in one of my Smarketing workshops.

Marketers say: Sales is ignoring Marketing.
When approached individually, salespeople are dismissive; when approached collectively, they are defensive. Salespeople come to meetings with a handful of dead leads waiting for their "gotcha moment". Marketing is guilty of a similar practice, bringing a list of promising leads that were fed into the sales funnel, only to be ignored and thus not producing results. The finger pointing begins from the word go, and before long, the meetings are little more than grievance-airing sessions, ones that nobody enjoys or looks forward to.

Proposed Solution:
To me, this is predominantly a mindset issue. One option is to adjust the frequency of Smarketing meetings. Additionally, have them facilitated by an outside party.

Comparing the Smarketing habits of growth organizations to their less successful counterparts, our past research, shows that most financially successful organizations have their sales and marketing teams meet formally and on a regular, perhaps even weekly, basis.

The diagram below clearly illustrates the enormous difference regular Sales – Marketing contact can make to the financial performance of a sales organization.

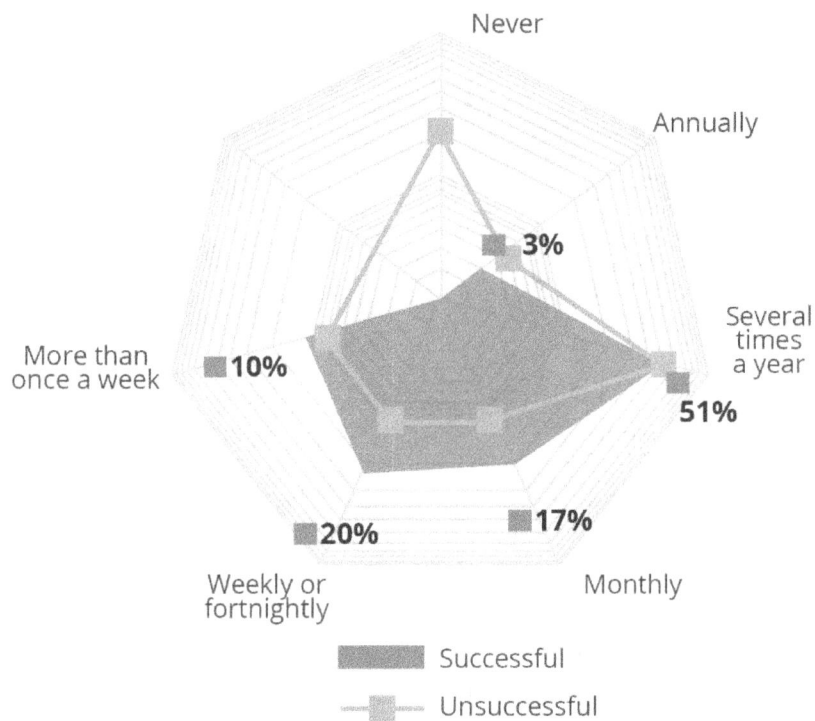

Frequency of Formal Sales and Marketing Team Meetings in Financially Successful vs Less Successful Companies

A final word on this matter:

I do not want you to think that I am attributing blame or glory to either Sales or Marketing.

I merely want to help both parties to come together as one team. One team that celebrates victories and bemoans losses, both small and large, together.

Nor does it mean that I am calling for an end to individual recognition, but when effective Smarketing is clearly responsible for a successful campaign then make sure that both departments are recognized for their respective contributions.

Try to improve camaraderie and mutual backslapping by making the recognition collective.

Chapter Takeaway

Even though – or perhaps because – it is increasingly difficult to define a hard and fast boundary between Sales and Marketing functions and their respective responsibilities, the pressures to perform that both teams find themselves constantly under ironically does not unite them.

Instead, it may be a source of friction between the teams. This friction is best countered through encouraging quality teamwork with well-defined common goals. That is what Smarketing is about.

We will explore that further in the next chapter.

Chapter 11:
Smarketing and The Productivity Trinity

First, dear Reader, please allow me to give you an advance notice: This chapter is a little more philosophical than some of the others. This is because in this chapter I am revealing some of my personal business beliefs and I'll be sharing part of my personal journey and how I finally arrived at Smarketing.

With over 20 years of B2B Sales and Marketing executive experience at some of the largest corporations on the planet, such as SONY, 3M, Canon and CSC, I have witnessed dozens of different approaches to improving sales results. Approaches that run the gamut from applying science, to applying plain hope. Some worked, some produced outcomes that were, shall we say, less than stellar.

Some years ago, I began to recognize certain patterns that struck me as strange in some of the more successful attempts. When I began to advise sales organizations, it became clear that these underlying patterns were not mere coincidence. Out of my observations I produced an important concept that for me now underpins Smarketing.

I call it The Productivity Trinity.

The Productivity Trinity recognizes that effective Smarketing is built upon the combination of People, Processes and Technology.

But not just any combination, as I will explain further down.

When The Productivity Trinity is not in place it leads precisely to the kind of situation that, according to Neil Rackham and Philip Kotler in the Harvard Business Review, "raises market-entry costs, lengthens sales cycles and increases cost of sales." See their famous paper, called "Ending The War Between Sales And Marketing" here: (http://hbr.org/2006/07/ending-the-war-between-sales-and-marketing/ar/1).

I agree wholeheartedly what these two experts said even back in 2006 when their paper was first released.

In fact, Smarketing is my solution to this persistent problem.

It promotes a movement away from "This is not my problem." to: "This is our problem.".

Smarketing does not promote doing away with the two specialist competency functions altogether. However, it is necessary to eliminate barriers to effective inter-departmental communication and collaboration. The goal is to build high-functioning partnerships that enhance sales health and outcomes.

So, it's not silos that should separate Sales from Marketing, yet we should not do away with boundaries altogether.

You may find it helpful to think of what should separate Sales from Marketing as something softer. Perhaps something like a semi-permeable membrane, or a transparent curtain, one that facilitates the movement of ideas between both departments but one through which each department can see what the other is doing, one through which positive and negative feedback can pass without a great deal of friction, and one where the functions are clearly defined, even though they may partially overlap.

If we want to achieve this outcome, we first need to understand that some small degree of tension between Sales and Marketing is healthy. The strategies that I cover in this book are not about eliminating this friction. Rather, they attempt to manage it to a point where it becomes constructive, highly effective, and eliminates Group Think, i.e. the tendency of a group of like-minded people to see things in the same way, killing diversity of thought.

Group Think leads to bad ideas going unchallenged, whereas input from a broad range of perspectives, combined with constructive friction (e. g. in the form of questioning and even pushback) is sometimes necessary for healthy decision-making.

Just as high-quality motor oil enhances performance in a motor vehicle, a good collaborative strategy can do the same for an organization. Neither eliminates friction altogether, but they dramatically reduce its negative effects. Collaborative strategies and high-quality motor oil are both compounds that, if applied in the right areas, will make the engine perform better, keeping the moving parts from grinding on each other.

This is what The Productivity Trinity is all about.

It makes sure that the grease goes in the right places. It focuses first and foremost on the People in an organization. Thereafter, it looks at the Processes and finally the Technology that they use:

People, Processes, and Technology, that is the right order of priority.

Extensive experience and research have proven time and again that this is a surefire way that organizations can build a lasting foundation upon which further collaborative strategies can be built. Implementing my method without regard to The Productivity Trinity puts the cart before the horse.

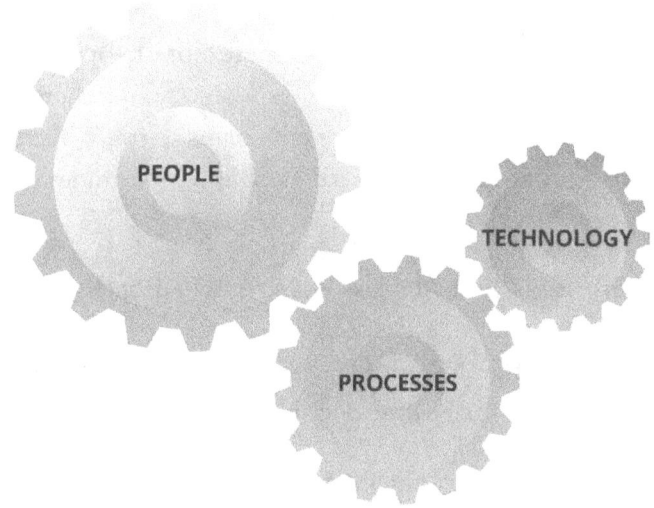

The Productivity Trinity
(By the way, the cogs are sized in order of my perception of their importance and business impact)

Let's now take a closer look at each of the three components of the Productivity Trinity.

Trinity Element 1: People Power

Let us not forget, when we are implementing any kind of collaborative strategy, we are dealing with human beings, which means we must also deal with all their thoroughly human imperfections and sensitivities.

The human element is not only the most crucial component of the Productivity Trinity; it is also the one most resistant to change.

It is for this reason that many would-be collaborators balk at the most crucial moment in the process – namely, addressing the counterproductive habits and mindsets of the individuals within the organization. Let's face the facts: effective Smarketing demands change that will touch upon nearly every facet of an organization. Those organizations that have most benefitted from Smarketing are those most willing to place everything – strategies, attitudes, perceptions, processes, and, yes, even corporate culture – under the microscope and possibly under the knife.

Since the term 'culture change' carries with it a host of negative connotations (especially for executives), I have found it best – and most successful – when talking about changing the way that functions interact within an organization to refer to the process as 'cultural alignment'.

No matter what you call it, as long as they go to the root of the challenge, small, manageable changes can have powerful effects from top to bottom within an organization. Each of the three steps in Smarketing addresses collaborative issues in this way. This is the reason that the organizations using the Method have enjoyed so much success. Rather than tackling the superficial symptoms of misalignment, we address the deeper causes, clearing the path for a more cooperative and prosperous future unencumbered with the collaborative issues of the past.

Nobody likes to be criticized but trying to circumvent the human element will never produce the kind of collaborative workplace in which everybody can thrive. The key throughout Smarketing is not to assign blame. Rather, it is about creating an environment in which collaboration is not only possible, but in which it occurs naturally.

This is not to say that less-than-desirable attitudes and behaviors are given a free pass. To use a sports analogy: We play the ball, not the man. The focus should be on giving the leadership team the tools that they need to improve inter-departmental relationships.

Trinity Element 2: Business Processes and Metrics

The next tier in the Productivity Trinity looks at the processes and metrics, particularly where those processes and metrics are applied to the points at which the two functions most often intersect. To be effective, any collaborative strategy must fearlessly navigate this territory, enhancing processes and developing joint metrics to continually improve the pipeline quality and quantity, and ultimately the sales outcome.

I have previously cited IDC's shocking statistic, but due to its significance it is worth repeating here:

> "Only 25 percent of sales leads and collateral that Marketing creates is ever used by Sales teams."
>
> - IDC

My own research and experience in the field confirm this statistic. When they look more closely, a surprising number of organizations recognize that the two departments are working at cross-purposes or with a large degree of duplication of effort.

For goal-alignment to be in place, Marketing's measure of success needs to be tied more closely to the Customer buying experience, to sales progress and to revenue results, not to lead generation alone.

Organizations that rely on a wide-mouthed sales lead pipeline – one in which Marketing is under substantial pressure to produce large numbers of leads – may be harming their bottom line by pressuring Marketing in this way to go for quantity over quality.

It is important for Marketing to understand that each one of the leads that are fed into the funnel translates into follow-up time spent on the part of Sales, even if it's only a quick touch to determine a lead's viability.

This can create a situation where Marketing is meeting its targets, but Sales is struggling to meet theirs, due to a significant amount of time spent chasing down unpromising opportunities.

We want Sales and Marketing to pull on the same rope on the same end, so there needs to be a set of agreed values, definitions, and, finally, metrics that both sides can live with. We want Sales to focus on selling and Marketing to concentrate on marketing. Anything other than this kind of cooperation represents a substantial financial risk in today's competitive markets.

Sales reps creating their own marketing collateral or modifying existing marketing collateral is a substantial waste of a salesperson's time. By the same token, it is equally unproductive to have Marketing people prepare collateral that will never make it into the Prospects' hands. Therefore, improving the relationship between Sales and Marketing can have demonstrable productivity-raising and revenue-boosting effects:

1) Salespeople will spend more of their time selling

2) Marketing will create more content that Sales will use

3) With the right type of collateral (collaboratively created in response to feedback) Sales will accelerate its deal velocity and increase closure rates

4) Marketing will enjoy a more productive relationship with Sales, and vice versa

5) Morale will improve, which in turn attracts and retains higher-performing talent

Once we have addressed the human element and have achieved consensus then the ensuing processes and metrics follow much more easily than they otherwise would, and the benefits of having everybody on the same page become indisputable.

Trinity Element 3: Technology

As I have not been shy about mentioning throughout this book, I approach technology with a degree of caution, and I advise others to do the same.

I caution against any approach that prioritizes technology solutions over the two other elements in the Productivity Trinity.

Don't just take my word for it. According to a comprehensive research report by Accenture and CSO Insights, called "Connecting The Dots On Sales Performance", which looked into the sales performance outcomes of sales and marketing automation technology implementations

https://dokumen.tips/amp/documents/accenture-connecting-dots-sales-performance.html

"An astounding 85 percent of organizations surveyed failed to increase revenue from technology deployments alone. And more than 90 percent were unable to reduce the time it takes to close a sale."

And even more damning:

"Fewer than 15 percent of organizations achieved improved win rates from implementing sales tools, mobile or otherwise."

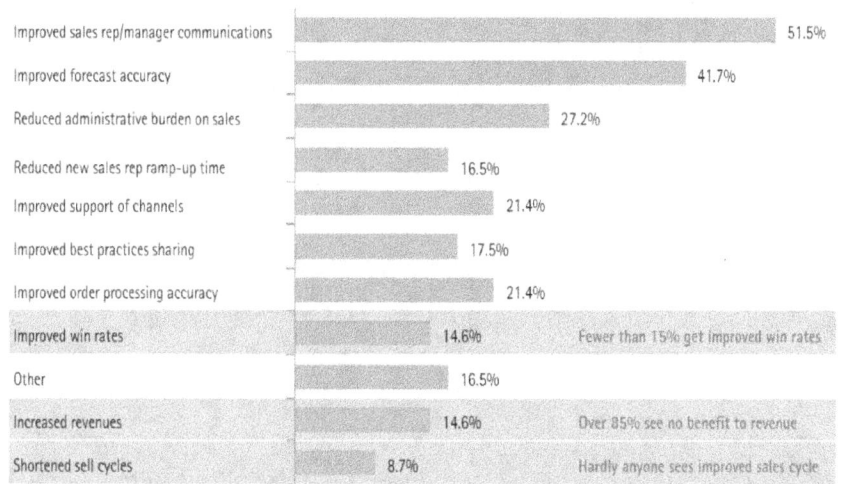

Accenture and CSO Insights' Research Report Says That Technology Alone Does Not Deliver Better Sales Performance

This does not mean that technology does not have a role to play in the Trinity and in Smarketing, but it is the third and final component in the Productivity Trinity. This is not because it is not important. No, it is listed here last because it helps to reinforce and maintain the structure that the other two elements of the Trinity have built. It comes last, but it is by no means least. In fact, technology can make information more accessible, it can facilitate dialogue and streamline well-thought-out business processes, but it should always be regarded as a tool, not as an end of its own.

Often, the challenge for tech-centric collaborators is the way that the solution is rolled out. End users often attempt to use the new technology in the same way that they did the old (often replicating and automating poorly performing processes). If it is the process that is at the root of the challenge, automation will only deliver flaws more quickly, not eradicate them for you. The same goes for data: no matter how sophisticated your new technology, feed it with incomplete, incorrect, or inconsistent (so-called 'dirty') data, and the results will inevitably disappoint. After all: bad data in = bad data out.

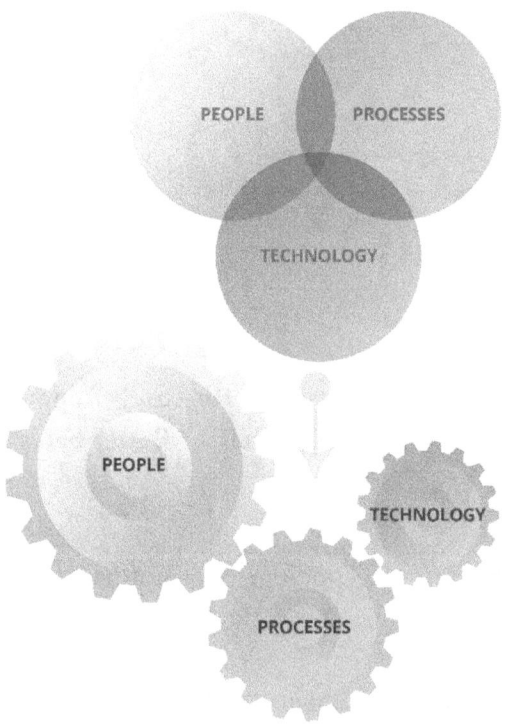

As I have stressed throughout this book, Smarketing takes a more fundamental approach to the short-term-istic ways that most organizations traditionally operate in, but its wide-reaching efficacy means that subsequent point solutions, such as sales training, that are applied after Smarketing is implemented, will work much more effectively, than before.

This is because when you get to a point where your teams want to work together, they will communicate more effectively and collaborate at a much deeper level than you could ever achieve through CRM or automation systems alone.

Above is an illustration that shows just how different the Smarketing approach is to the mere implementation of, say, collaboration technology.

At the top you see the typical Venn diagram that technology integrators often use when describing their focus areas. The three equally sized circles do not really match up to the way that many collaboration solutions are typically implemented.

The reality is this: A faithful representation of technology implementations today would feature a Technology circle that would dwarf the other two.

We know that technology alone is not the answer, it never was. A tool is just a tool, whereas it's the skills of the craftsman that produces the result.

Finally, under the banners of 'multi-channel strategy' and 'content curation' too many marketing departments automate intending to broadcast as far and wide as possible. Automation tools may well allow for this amplification and broadcasting of, say, an organization's online presence, but the organizations that are finding new technology the most effective are those using the latest tools to target in sophisticated ways smaller, more focused groups of qualified and motivated Prospects.

No more "spray & pray".

World-leading organizations consistently use technology like a scalpel, not like a flame thrower.

Chapter Takeaway

My Smarketing Productivity Trinity recognizes the importance of an approach that puts People first, Processes second, and Technology third. In my observation, this approach is the only way to guarantee that would-be collaborators will see their efforts rewarded with success.

Chapter 12: Implementing Smarketing

In this chapter I will outline the exact steps that my clients have successfully taken to align their sales and marketing teams for higher output across the board.

This is not to say that all the minutiae of these strategies apply equally in all cases, or specifically to your organization. Rather, they represent the range of options and challenge-specific solutions that I have found lead to the kind of outcomes that my clients call me in for.

In their fifth annual edition of insights and trends from over 4,100 marketing leaders worldwide, called "The State of Marketing 2020", Salesforce.com reported that only 52 percent of respondents say they share common goals and metrics between Sales and Marketing teams. In the same report Salesforce.com also emphasizes the importance of good inter-team collaboration, i.e. Smarketing, saying:

"Sales and Marketing alignment is hardly a new concept. But as increasingly sophisticated customer experiences elevate consumers' expectations, standards are rising for business purchases, too. Therefore, it's critical for all sales and marketing to march in tandem."

https://www.salesforce.com/blog/2018/12/introducing-fifth-state-of-marketing-report.html

So, how to get started with Smarketing?

Through personal experience I have found that most people do not like to be told that they are doing something wrong. It just leads to defensive behavior, particularly if it comes from someone external to the organization.

Instead, it is far more helpful if you can discover for yourself the opportunities for improvement. It is even better if you can then take the initiative and raise your personal and professional brand in the process, too.

After all, no two organizations are the same, and they often are at very different stages of maturity, in terms of the Smarketing spectrum. Some are just starting out on their collaborative journey, while others may already be well on their way.

For that reason, I have developed a quick **self-assessment test**, which is available free of charge at peterstrohkorb.com/smarketing-test

This free test answers some very practical questions for you:

- **"How closely are our Sales and Marketing teams aligned, really?"**

- **"Where do we still have gaps to fill?"**

- **Where do we have quick win-win opportunities?**

Visit peterstrohkorb.com/smarketing-test and try the Smarketing Test now. You'll find answers to the above questions in just about 5 minutes, and you will also receive your personal Smarketing Score.

After you have completed the Smarketing Test you might be ready to dip your toe further into the water.

The question on your lips might be this:

How do you get started with Smarketing?

The real breakthrough begins with a dialog that allows the stakeholders to dream and to imagine what a more collaborative future could bring to the organization and what it could mean for the individuals involved.

It is for this reason that I have developed a flexible toolkit that has helped my clients to baseline and benchmark their Smarketing Maturity as a first step.

Then, it provides my clients with the exact tools and processes to improve their organizational Smarketing Maturity and subsequently to accelerate their sales velocity.

There is one prerequisite to success, though:

I have found that inter-departmental change rarely works if it is not sponsored by the senior leadership team.

It is for that reason that I recommend you start with a complimentary Executive Discovery Session.

Book me in to introduce the Smarketing concept, outline the benefits, transparently answer your questions, and detail some specific case studies for you.

Armed with that information, you may then decide to move on to a Smarketing workshop where I will support you as an independent, external and impartial intermediary who helps both parties to see the new, collaborative future not only as workable, but as desirable, instead of as some sort of forced-labor imposition.

In the workshop your teams will likely discover that they would like to measure objectively the level of collaboration between the teams today, so that progress can be measured and monitored. In the same workshop your teams will start to identify the first specific collaboration opportunities, which will build early excitement about where this initiative could take them.

The Smarketing workshop sets the scene for the formal rollout of Smarketing into your organization.

As you will see on the next page, Smarketing then rolls out in individual steps that each adds increasing insight, value and results.

I call this implementation methodology *The OneTEAM Method*®, which is also the title of my previous book, available on Amazon.

On the next page is a high-level illustration of how The OneTEAM Method® brings Smarketing into an organization.

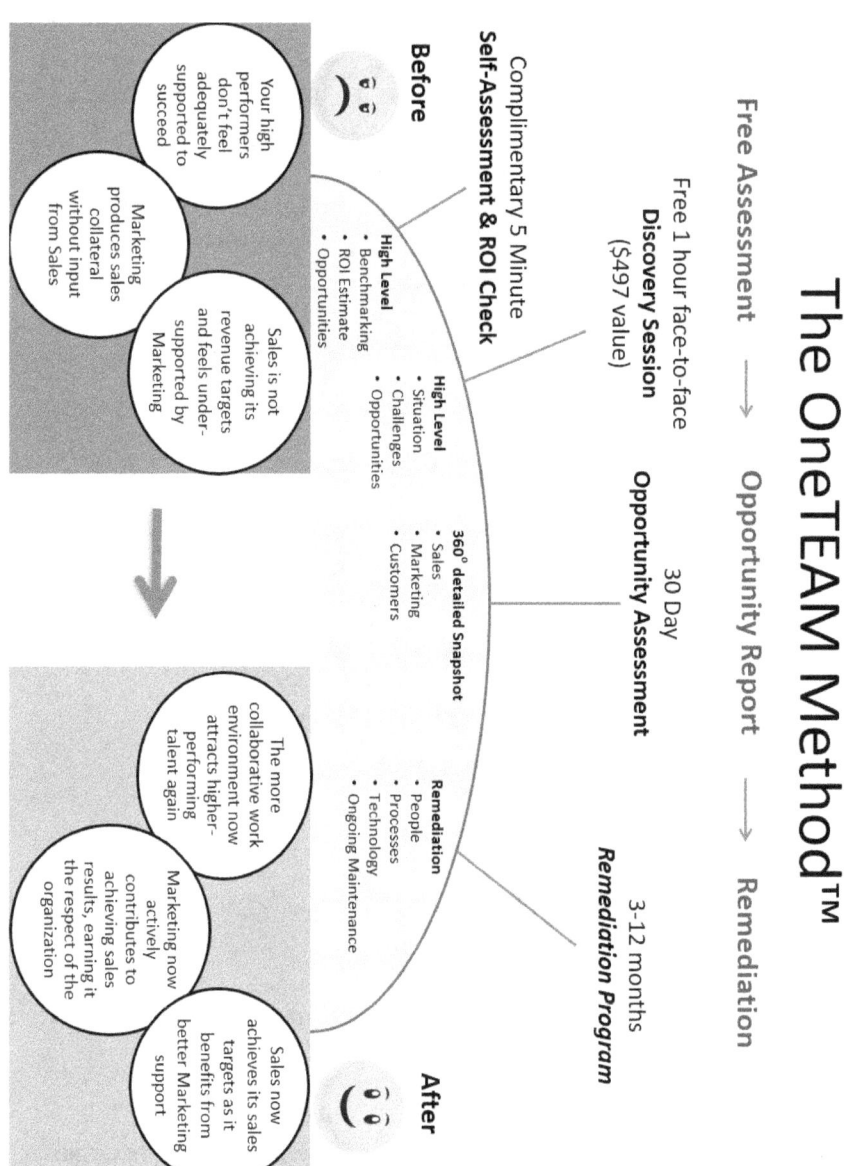

How to implement Smarketing with the OneTEAM Method™

Let us now look at a more granular level how you can implement Smarketing into your organization.

We do this by taking our clients through a proven 5-step process.

The first three steps are to gather important insights, which are then used in the Planning Step, thus giving the Implementation Step the highest possible likelihood of success.

Together, they look as follows:

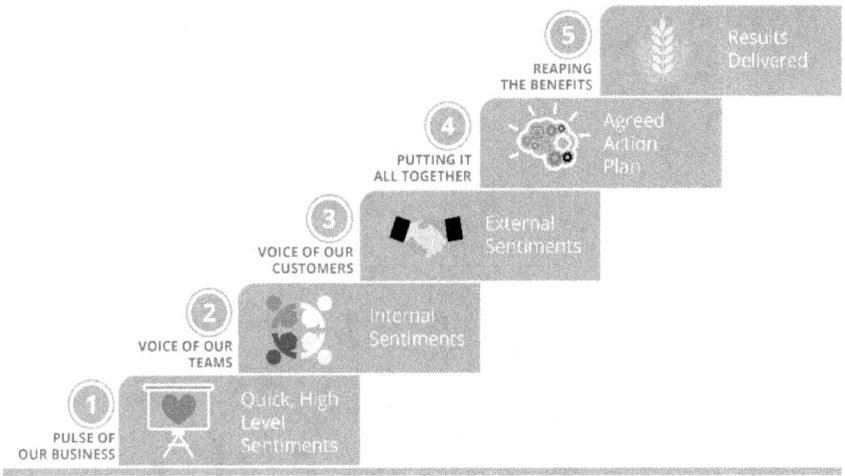

The Smarketing Implementation Steps

The order and the objective of each step are extremely important, so let us go through them in more detail next.

Steps 1-3: Benchmarking Your Smarketing Maturity

The first step in the Method is to assess the current state of Smarketing Maturity within your organization.

This is further detailed in the **Smarketing Step 1 brochure,** which is available for free download at https://peterstrohkorb.com/smarketing.

Step 1 is themed "The Pulse of Our Business".

What questions does Step 1 answer?

- What business potential can better collaboration achieve for us?
- How well do our current collaborative processes work for us?
- Which best-practice collaboration processes are we still missing?
- What are our challenges to improve our Sales & Marketing effectiveness?
- What is our Smarketing Maturity Score (details below)?

It is a fast and inexpensive way to start a conversation in your business about current collaboration effectiveness and the business benefits if it were to be improved.

In short: This first step will unearth your internal Smarketing Maturity and show you the way forward towards more sales and a superior customer experience.

More information is available at https://peterstrohkorb.com/smarketing.

Step 2 is called "The Voice of Our Teams".

This is because we unearth the true sentiments of your sales and marketing people in a neutral, safe, and unencumbered environment.

This insight will arm you to understand the underlying issues and sometimes inter-personal frictions that can affect your Smarketing success down the track if they were to be left unchecked.

Step 3 is called "The Voice of Our Customers"

It gives you a 360-degree view of the underlying Smarketing-related issues by capturing the sentiment, perspectives and – importantly – genuine feedback from perhaps the most important set of your stakeholders: Your Customers.

These sentiments are then both qualified and quantified in your **Smarketing Maturity Score,** which uncovers the underlying issues, challenges and opportunities bringing Smarketing into your organization.

The Smarketing Score is expressed in the range of 1 to 100 points.

- It is our best-practice metric of your Marketing & Sales collaboration quality

- It benchmarks how your teams perceive the level of their collaboration today

- It is a leading indicator of the collaboration quality in your business

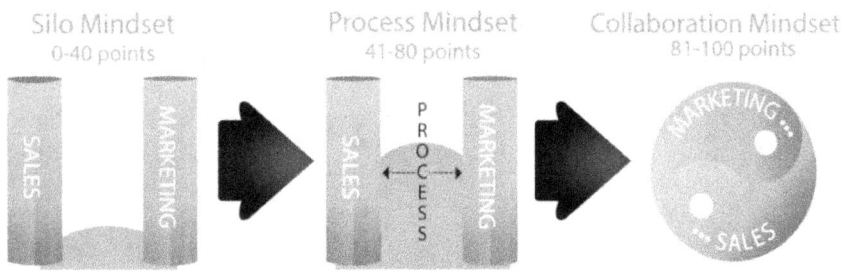

The Smarketing Score Attributed to The Maturity Stages

For illustration purposes I have pasted a sample score below.

It clearly shows the spread of alignment (or misalignment) in terms of lowest, highest, and median Smarketing scores in a sample organization.

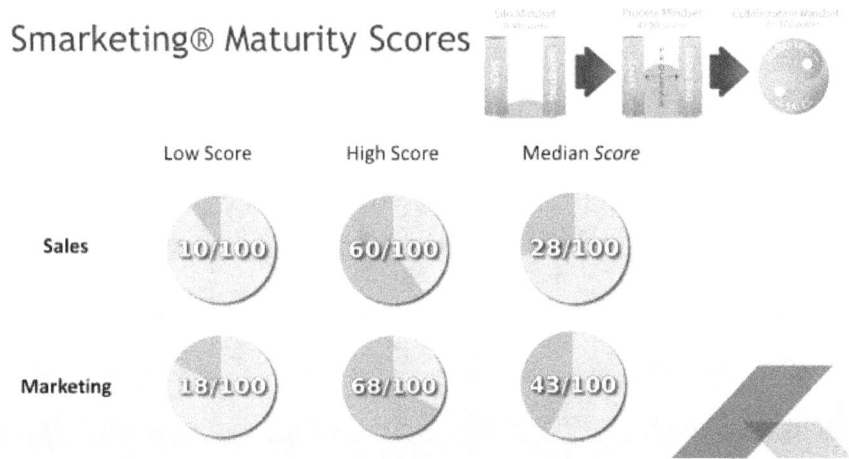

An Example of a Smarketing Maturity Score Across Teams

Oftentimes, this is the first time a quantitative analysis of an organization's Sales and Marketing collaboration has been undertaken. For that reason, it is not unusual for the results to be thought-provoking and to stimulate robust debate, which is a sign that the idea is sinking in.

Step 4: A Co-Created Action Plan

This is where the rubber hits the road. It is extremely important that your Smarketing implementation plan is welcomed and even embraced by all involved. This is to avoid active and passive resistance and to ensure that the plan is implemented as quickly and as effectively as possible.

It is for this reason that I strongly recommend you do not limit the planning stage to your executive team only. My recommendation is to actively involve your middle management and even your frontline staff so that everyone feels they are part of the solution and that it is not something that is being imposed on them.

Trust me, the results will be that much more impressive if you co-create the implementation plan with all stakeholders involved. Don't' worry, I have a method to manage this process effectively.

So, together, we will devise your organization-specific action plan and roadmap.

More information is available at
https://peterstrohkorb.com/smarketing.

At a high level, this can include details on the following measures:

Compel Sales to provide feedback on Marketing's outputs

There is an important distinction to be made here. We want to enable Sales to critique – but not to criticize – Marketing. Also, this critique is applied to Marketing's output, not to Marketing itself.

This distinction must be upheld if we are to get away from the counterproductive environment of finger-pointing and mutual recrimination. For Smarketing to work, it has to begin with a clear understanding of the difference between constructive feedback and unconstructive criticism.

Sales' feedback to Marketing is often not encouraged, perhaps because it can lean towards being "safe" and generalist in nature, rather being than specific to collaboration.

Or, it may be directed at a specific person, rather than at a solvable business issue, or simply because the CRM system does not cater to it beyond the reporting on sales leads follow-up.

To this point, whatever feedback there is from Sales often comes from the more vocal and perhaps more frustrated sales reps.

Opinions of this kind can become confrontational and hurtful. This is often the result of the traditionally one-directional nature of traditional feedback channels.

Frustrations can build up over time, and eventually, maybe even inevitably, manifest themselves in unpleasant outbursts.

It is for this reason that your Sales and Marketing feedback loops need to promote communication in both directions.

Since feedback channels in poorly aligned organizations often tend to over-represent the voice of a vocal minority (e.g., the "hero sales reps"), there needs to be a mechanism in place to encourage constructive feedback from all reps, regardless of their performance, seniority or their geographic location.

Besides, I have repeatedly found that some of the best ideas come from those who speak the softest. People in remote branches far away from head office and those that are quieter and more reserved by nature often need more than just a seat at the table; they need to be encouraged to offer their opinions and ideas.

Regardless of their location (i.e. whether they are based at head office or in the farthest regions of the organization, whether they are inside sales, outside sales, direct sales or indirect sales) give each and every sales rep a formal channel that allows them to constructively critique the content and support that they are receiving from Marketing. Again, it is important that this empowerment doesn't translate to fruitless broad-brush criticism.

Ask sales reps to start rating Marketing's output on a simple scale of 1 to 5. Optionally, they can also make suggestions as to how marketing content can be improved to better suit the specific ways in which it is being used. They can use this opportunity to ask for additional support, to speak openly and frankly about what has worked, has not worked, is working, or is not working. They can also relay back to Marketing how they are using or would like to use the content and how it can be improved to become more useful or impactful in that context.

Make sure to make these suggestions and ratings highly visible. To be effective this process must be as transparent as possible from the outset. This transparency should be universal, making little distinctions of rank or location.

No longer is direct feedback restricted to the vocal minority of head office-based sales reps or to the ones that are located physically near Marketing. Instead, every rep, regardless of rank and location, now has an equal opportunity to speak to Marketing and, perhaps more importantly, to be heard.

The kind of difference this kind of feedback mechanism can make in a very short time is often nothing short of remarkable. Sales reps who feel appreciated, who feel their opinions are of value, often become key players in the collaborative process.

Sales benefit from the ability to provide qualitative feedback on the entire array of support that it is receiving from Marketing (i.e. more than just the sales leads), as well as being able to suggest improvements and even new initiatives. Marketing benefits from the mining of previously untapped potential. Feedback from Sales soon becomes a valuable resource, one that helps Marketing to hone content to a fine point.

This is not to mean that Marketing will now slavishly follow whatever Sales suggests. Instead, Marketing benefits from the feedback that it is now receiving from the entire sales force on an ongoing basis and finally has the information that it needs to make better-informed decisions on how they can support the sales force more effectively Crucially, as we'll see in the next step, Marketing too has an important role and a strong voice in the method.

Encourage Marketing to Respond to Sales' Feedback

I feel I need to start my discussion here with an important distinction: Marketing is compelled to react to the feedback, but that does not mean they are beholden to Sales.

In many organizations, Marketing is the sender and Sales the receiver: Marketing throws sales material in the form of brochures, white papers, blogs, and leads 'over the fence', and Sales is expected to make the most (ideally without complaint) of this material. I have frequently stressed the importance of a two-way dialogue between Sales and Marketing that gives each department equal footing, so it is important to highlight the fact that Marketing is in no way shut out of, or a victim of the feedback loop. It is only natural for Marketing to defend the quality of its collateral and its sales leads. The feedback that Marketing receives is never intended to be the final word. It merely provides the transparency in terms of the sales force's sentiments that Marketing has hitherto lacked. A constructive feedback channel that is open in both directions allows both departments to make informed decisions.

However, the feedback from Sales would soon stop if Marketing did not respond in some palpable way to the new feedback. So, in order to be a truly collaborative system of feedback, Marketing must be compelled to respond to Sales' feedback. If sales reps' feedback disappeared into a black hole without response from Marketing, the feedback would not only soon stop again, but the teams would likely go back to their previous modus operandi of mutual distrust and animosity – and we know where that leads.

I have found nothing dams up collaborative channels faster than Sales offering unprecedented levels of feedback to Marketing without perceiving any tangible change in the type or quality of marketing collateral or sales leads.

For the relationship to be even remotely successful, sales reps need to feel that their feedback forms a crucial part of the cross-functional dialogue.

Help Salespeople to see that Marketing is responding to their feedback

If Sales are investing time and effort to provide feedback to Marketing, then it will be critical to ongoing success that they see their feedback make a tangible difference in the collateral and leads that Marketing is generating.

This does not mean that Sales' feedback is must-do gospel; after all, we are looking to achieve tighter integration, not to create a master/slave relationship. It does, however, mean that Sales' feedback is a valuable source of market insight and that it should be regarded and treated as such.

The way that Smarketing achieves this is through mutual consent and bargaining between sales and marketing teams. When outlining the strategy within your own organization, it is helpful to create something of a tit-for-tat dialogue.

The solution needs to feel like a win-win, and, for the sake of a win, both sides of the debate are usually willing to compromise somewhat. As soon as you have reached a stage where agreement can be reached along the lines of Marketing will do X, if Sales will do Y, then you are well on your way to finding mutually agreeable common ground.

My experience has reinforced my long-held belief that as long as the feedback that Marketing is receiving from Sales is constructive, Marketing's response tends to be constructive as well. The same can be said for unemotional feedback. No matter who is on the giving or the receiving end of feedback, emotional delivery tends to produce an equally emotional response.

Given the chance to evaluate specific, constructive, and unemotional feedback from Sales rationally, Marketing can be compelled via joint metrics and common objectives to respond in kind. The kind of feedback channel I am describing here allows Sales to feel and see that they are being heard and that their opinions are valued. On the flip side it enables Marketing access to the precise kinds of information that can make their collateral and leads not only reflect the wants and needs of Sales but as a consequence also make them more successful.

Creating proximity is a great way to break down barriers. Bringing Sales and Marketing together regularly and, if possible, face-to-face can make a huge difference.

The trick is to find the organizationally specific balance between meeting too often and meeting too little. In my own research, I found that a particularly statistically significant difference between successful and less-successful organizations was the high percentage of financially less-successful organizations that admitted to 'never' having meetings that bring both Sales and Marketing to the one table.

The more successful organizations have learned that frequent, structured, and mediated meetings are a good way to engage both departments in productive dialogue, especially in the early stages of Smarketing implementation.

For the feedback channels to be effective, meetings must not be grievance free-for-alls. Take the temperature early in these meetings and seek ways to keep things conversational and, as I highlighted above, constructive and unemotional (e.g. "it would work better for us if…" rather than "this is useless because…"). You need to show as early as possible that negative or hurtful outbursts and tantrums will not be rewarded.

It often helps to have a neutral mediator like me in charge of proceedings who can make sure that the workshop focuses on achieving positive outcomes and that finger-pointing, and chest thumping are kept to a respectable minimum.

Now, in a truly collaborative workplace, Marketing and Sales should be self-initiating constructive meetings. The mediator's role should shrink as Smarketing becomes entrenched in the organization.

While having regular meetings is clearly important, the quality of the meetings is even more so. Constructive and collaborative meetings are a direct result of the openly cooperative mindset of those who attend them.

This, to me, is the real differentiator.

If your Smarketing meetings are to be successful (i.e. if is all to result in a more collaborative workplace), then it is important that Sales experiences the fact that Marketing is really listening to them (i.e. not just politely smiling and nodding) and that it is following up with agreed actions.

This is the purpose of compelling Marketing to respond to the feedback from Sales.

The best way for Marketing to show Sales that they are listening is to respond to Sales' feedback with tangibly better and more responsive support.

This may not happen overnight, but by trying to be better, Marketing will eventually hit upon something that Sales will use to good effect. Trial and error should not be avoided. On the contrary, the newly collaborative environment should be one in which making mistakes is not only tolerated but accepted, maybe even welcomed.

Building more effective communication channels begins with the effort, not the results. As numerous studies have shown, the best way to learn is from making mistakes. As long as each mistake is only made once, is learned from, and is not repeated. I am not talking about multi-million-dollar mistakes here. I am talking about learned experiences, what some change management consultants have dubbed 'Action Learning' – sophisticated trial and error experiments, really.

At a high level we want to embark on a collaboration trajectory that takes us from conversation to trust, to joint decisions, to shared responsibility, to personal accountability and finally to collective ownership of the business outcome

Once feedback channels are established and nurtured, it is time to introduce joint metrics, definitions and overlapping responsibilities. While the entrance to the pipeline is the most important intersection (and the first one you'll want to build shared definitions and metrics around) goal alignment, and to some degree compensation as well, will eventually need to take both ends of the sales pipeline into account. If Marketing is only compensated according to the top end of the sales pipeline or funnel, then this fuels complacency and exacerbates the quantity over quality issue that would-be collaborators should always try to avoid.

Any time that processes or metrics are under the microscope, it is crucial to make sure that there is agreement between the parties as to what, precisely, is being measured.

The goal is to eventually have an integrated process that centers on the Buyer's journey all the way from the initial Buyer contact to the closing handshake. You can reasonably expect that customer experience will also improve commensurately with the improved Smarketing.

The hardest part may well turn out to be determining to what degree Marketing is accountable for selling. In most organizations, Marketing is measured according to the quantity of sales leads that it generates and then passes on to Sales.

This leads to at least three challenges:

1) Lead quantity will trump quality, and blame can be shifted from Marketing to the 'incompetent' salespeople, who are unable to close out the sales leads that Marketing has supplied.

2) Understandably frustrated with this process, Sales will reject a staggering percentage of Marketing leads as inadequate. If Marketing performance is assessed according to Sales Accepted Leads, this can quickly sour the relationship and hinder productive communication.

3) Salespeople who are struggling to meet their targets will often gravitate towards only the highest quality and most short-term leads. It is only natural, prevailing wisdom says, to go for the bird in the hand, leaving the birds in the bush to other, less-experienced sales reps who may struggle mightily to reach their targets. This kind of system can lead to huge numbers of expensively procured sales leads going to waste.

The next step, then, is to compel Marketing to respond in a transparent and open way to the feedback it receives from Sales. It is important not only that Sales can see that Marketing is listening to them, but also that it can directly witness how Marketing is responding to the feedback with tangibly improved and more responsive support.

By the way, this new collaborative environment should also be one where making mistakes is not only tolerated but accepted, maybe even welcomed, as long as each mistake is only made once learned from.

Also, I am not talking about multi-million-dollar mistakes. I am talking about tactical learned experiences. Some management consultants refer to this as "Action Learning" where we are taking people or teams from initial conversation to agreement, then trust, then decision making, then group responsibility, to individual accountability and finally to outcomes ownership. But it does not need to be as complicated as it may sound here in consultant-speak.

For example, it is entirely acceptable to try a few different versions of a brochure with different customers or in different markets to see which one has the highest impact. Equally, there may well be a disagreement even between salespeople regarding the efficacy of a campaign or promotion. In those cases, it should not be a big challenge to run multiple variants on the same theme in different market segments to determine which ones work best. So, I suppose if we substituted the word "mistakes" with "learning experience" then everybody should know what is meant.

Rather than broadly negative feedback (e.g., "Marketing's sales leads and content are useless"), each and every interaction should become an exercise in enhancing the organizational performance and the customer experience.

If necessary, Marketing and Sales may need to re-adjust their messaging in order to more effectively draw in those customers who are in the organization's target sweet spot.

Goal alignment, and to some degree compensation as well, must take both ends of the sales pipeline into account. If Marketing is only compensated according to the top end of the sales pipeline or funnel, then this fuels complacency, and it exacerbates the quantity-over-quality issue that I mentioned above.

Although a reward structure that is revised towards sales outcomes is rarely something that Marketing departments will greet with great enthusiasm, having take-home pay adjusted so that there are rewards for Marketing's offering of higher quality leads and better content for Sales can be in everybody's best interest.

This kind of alignment needs to begin with a collective understanding of terminology. True alignment of processes definition means that not only is 'revenue' a term with agreed-upon parameters, so too is lead generation, nurturing and management, which can be established with the aid of lead-scoring. There are quite a number of lead scoring methods readily available, and most CRM vendors offer these techniques off the shelf.

To me, it matters less which of these my clients choose to deploy, than it does having a high level of agreement between Sales and Marketing. The fact that they are collaborating is more important to me than which tool they use.

The Method helps the teams to understand why and how they should collaborate. As tempted as you might be to force success upon your organization, resist the urge to make such an attempt. Buy-in from every level should make the implementation, while not easy, at least somewhat natural and more even handed. Forcing people, processes or technologies into situations or places in which they don't fit will get you nowhere, fast.

Build A Virtuous Cycle of Collaboration

When we talk about building and maintaining a virtuous circle of collaboration, it is only the latter (maintaining the circle) that will guarantee long-term success. Allow old habits and mindsets to creep back into the relationship and you will find yourself precisely back where you started.

To avoid slipping back into bad habits I highly recommend that organizations consider installing a dedicated person or team responsible for improving and maintaining Smarketing.

My research shows that sales force effectiveness is stronger in organizations in which both Sales and Marketing report to a single capable executive.

It shows that the closer the ties are between Sales and Marketing, the higher their success rate.

Be extremely diligent when assigning the task of overseeing Smarketing to anybody in-house.

Neutrality is extremely important; the CMO/VP of Marketing or the CSO/VP of Sales should not feel as though an internal stakeholder with their own vested interests is dictating to them. Keep in mind also that lower ranking people often do not feel comfortable expressing their true opinions and ideas to senior executives. They fear that too much limelight could be a CLM, career-limiting move" for them.

Finally, remember that the customer, of course, is also a member of the collaborative circle. Customers on the Buyer's journey are looking for advisors, but they are also looking for collaborators.

In this way, the customer is the most important arbiter of successful Smarketing. All partnerships should aim to improve customer-facing aspects of both functions.

Attracting and retaining today's most desirable customers will become easier the longer you are able to maintain a virtuous circle of collaboration within your organization. When it comes to maintaining the collaborative environment and practices that typify the aligned organization, then the third element in the Trinity, i.e. Technology becomes crucial.

Step 5: Implementing Your Smarketing Action Plan

The key to a successful implementation is to gain buy-in from all stakeholders. If you have successfully co-created your Smarketing Action Plan, then the implementation should be far easier than if it were imposed on the organization from the top.

My advice is to use project management principles to keep the implementation on track and everybody informed on progress. Determine who will do what, by when, measure, manage and report on progress to keep the momentum going.

Ask my help if you think it could be useful.

Chapter Takeaway

We learned that Smarketing can start small, e.g. it can initially be applied to just one specific deal or to just one account, and then grow from there before you move on to eventually streamlining your entire Revenue Funnel. You can choose where you want to get started. The key is to just make a start somewhere.

Whether you are taking the first step of your collaborative journey or the last one, my team and I will be happy to help you through the Smarketing steps and to ensure that you obtain the best results possible.

What is more, we will make sure that the results last.

Chapter 13:
Various Client Success Stories

So far, we have heard about the concept and the methods behind Smarketing. Let us now look at what Smarketing has achieved for real-world client organizations.

I have listed below some examples for your reference:

A National Electricity Provider

I was introduced to the CEO of this national electricity and gas retailer through a mutual acquaintance. The CEO had been in this new role for less than a year, coming from an EVP position at a large telco.

The CEO and I met for breakfast and we talked about the challenges he was discovering in his new role. He mentioned that, although he could not quite put his finger on the exact reason, it seemed to him that his sales and marketing teams were not operating in unison.

On further examination it transpired that his organization had a centralized marketing team, a direct sales force, a reseller channel and two call centers, one in-bound service desk and one out-bound BDR team, located in two separate geographies. Customers are in B2C and B2B, comprising households and businesses.

After a few minutes of talking with the CEO it became clear that there seemed to be no unifying strategy (or metrics) between Sales and Marketing in this organization, and that whatever success had been achieved was largely due to the heroic efforts of a small number of individuals on both the Marketing and on the Sales side.

In other words, collaboration was not baked into the business culture.

I mentioned to the CEO that our research had conclusively shown that organizations that have Marketing and Sales report into a single, appropriately qualified, executive were more likely to experience financial growth than those that had separate Heads of Marketing and of Sales.

On the strength of this recommendation the CEO decided to recruit a brand-new VP of Sales & Marketing, and to roll out Smarketing as part of the new VP's business transformation initiative.

Although this delayed the roll out of our Smarketing by a few months it was the right thing to do in the interest of the client organization, its CEO, and its customers.

The newly recruited VP of Sales & Marketing started in January and we agreed to implement the assessment Steps 1 and 2 of Smarketing from February.

What we found was significant.

We assessed the staff sentiments in terms of their sales and marketing collaboration and found that they were largely disengaged from the organization, and that both their morale and their loyalty to the business were very low. Further, the call centers were not outsourced, but they were situated in another state.

Separated by geographical distance the call center staff felt that they were treated by head office like second-class citizens, that their opinions were not requested, nor valued, and that they were perceived as mere robots who weren't allowed to think for themselves.

I presented the findings of Smarketing Steps 1 and 2 to the CEO and to the Sales & Marketing VP in one session in March. They were shocked at the revelation of how far apart their sales and marketing teams were.

Not only did the Smarketing scores show a huge gap (we expected that it would be large), but we also found that even within the sales and the marketing functions there were huge discrepancies.

Put these results together and it turned out that there were individuals within the sales force and the marketing team that had formed informal relationships that helped them to be more effective than others. But they were by far the exception.

Once the presentation came to the staff verbatims from our Step 2 work some of the truth really came out. You see, Smarketing ensures the anonymity of its participants, which makes them feel more comfortable to be open and frank, and to say what they really think. And, boy, did they let rip. They were very frank.

But the reaction of the CEO was exemplar.

He said: "Oh my god, I had no idea how bad this situation is. Had I known; I would have done something about this much sooner. OK, the buck stops with me. We will fix this."

I was relieved, because no matter how much you prepare senior executives for bad news, at times they may prefer to blame the method or the messenger, rather than admitting to a problem existing in their organization.

So, this CEO was open to the feedback, and he was ready and willing to act on it.

We rolled out the other steps of Smarketing over the next few months, fostering and formalizing bi-directional and collaborative relationships between the sales force, the call centers, and the marketing team.

But in the afternoon of the last day of June that year disaster struck.

A huge telco outage affected the outbound call center, which meant that the call center staff were unable to make outbound calls.

Had this situation occurred back in February, the call center staff would have given up their post and headed for their homes for the day as the outage happened in the late afternoon close to the end of their shift.

Here is what happened instead:

The call center staff rallied around their manager and agreed to continue to make calls to the company's clients and prospects **using their personal cell phones** in order to reach the sales quota that they were so tantalizingly close to reaching.

Can you see how that is a 180-degree turn-around in their attitude from just a few months earlier, back in February?

That is real staff engagement.

But the good news did not stop there.

With this level of team commitment, the company achieved its best sales month ever, just three months later!

Everybody made their bonuses, the CEO was happy, the shareholders were happy, and the business keeps going from strength to strength.

There is one more surprise:

A year later, the CEO moved on, and the Sales & Marketing VP was promoted to the CEO position. She still heads up the organization today.

Afterwards, this is what the now CEO said at the time, when asked whether she would recommend Smarketing:

"I absolutely recommend it!"
- CEO

You can see the entire CEO testimonial and her video at peterstrohkorb.com/testimonials,
or go straight to YouTube at https://youtu.be/j-6d6K5rkOc

A Professional Services Startup Business

This example shows that Smarketing is not just for big business.

My client at the time was a two-year-old startup with 16 employees in the professional services sector. This organization is an energy efficiency advisory firm with offices across two major capital cities. It is funded by two venture capital firms and was expected to grow rapidly.

When I met the CEO his marketing and sales teams were not collaborating effectively across its two main locations. The sales force was still running with campaigns that Marketing had long discontinued, and Marketing's new campaigns were not resonating with the sales force or with the target market as communication with Prospects and Customers was inconsistent.

Therefore, sales performance was suffering, and the company's financiers were getting anxious about the expected revenue and profit growth.

After a short discussion with the CEO we agreed to implement a fast-tracked version of Smarketing across the two locations over a six-week period.

In the subsequent two weeks after implementing our program the company achieved the following results:

Revenue Outcome: They achieved the same revenue in this two-week period as they had made in the previous six months!

Contracts Outcome:
They signed their largest customer yet

PR Outcome:
Won a prestigious new "marquee" customer

Pipeline Outcome:
Opened up a large upsell opportunity

Innovation Outcome:
Won a major contract for an innovative solar project

Profit Outcome:
Improved their sales margins

Marketing Outcome:
Tripled the size of their marketing database

And last, not least:

Investor Outcome:
The financiers regained faith in the CEO and in their investment. They are now confident that their money is safe and providing a good return.

Here is what the CEO said afterwards:

"Thanks to Peter, we were able to improve our margins, move into a higher customer segment and record the same amount of sales revenue in two weeks that had previously taken us six months to generate."

- CEO

You can see what else he said on my website at
https://peterstrohkorb.com/testimonials ,
or go straight to YouTube at
https://www.youtube.com/watch?v=x88EsytcbGs&t=11s

A Multinational Logistics and Freight Forwarding Company

As often happens, I was introduced to this client by a mutual contact. One of the company's Directors and I made an appointment to meet with me and to discuss their business challenges. The subsidiary had acquired a string of smaller local freight forwarders to give it a broader geographical branch presence across all states of the country.

The Board of Directors wanted the integration of the new businesses to be accomplished as quickly as possible in order to leverage the expected productivity gains and to maintain the very high standard of customer experience that this company had prided itself on. However, the acquired businesses still had the original founders and owners in place who continued to manage these branches as though they were still their own businesses. Something had to be done to unify the organization into one high-performing culture.

The Director chose to engage me to accelerate their inter-team collaboration. We first agreed on our approach and then deployed a customized version of Smarketing. We ran two separate program streams: One for the executive team and branch managers, and one for all other staff.

Our intervention only took six weeks, during which we conducted several assessments, seminars, and workshops.

The results were spectacular:

- Inter-branch collaboration improved after just two weeks!
- Staff engagement followed closely behind
- Customer satisfaction was back to the target levels within six weeks
- The financial performance of the company finally is hitting the sales forecast
- This national freight company is now going from strength to strength!

To see what one of the Board Directors said about working with me afterwards, see the video at https://peterstrohkorb.com/testimonials , or go straight to YouTube at https://youtu.be/pakbnlNivR4

A Multinational Corporation in The Industrial Technology Sector

In this case, I do not need to tell you the story of this company. The CEO told me in his own words what happened:

"I contacted Peter initially to discuss my perception that my Sales and Marketing teams were not collaborating as well as they could. Peter challenged that the issues were not isolated to these two functions. In consultation, Peter proposed a course of action to re-unite and realign my executive leadership team towards a common goal: Our customers.

Within a very short period of time my executive team not only agreed to collaborate more effectively, but they also agreed on how they would do so and put in place measures to make the collaboration part of our culture.

The results of Peter's good work have assisted our organization to face its revenue goals with confidence and as one team."

- Signed by the Managing Director

The background is that the head office had given this organization an ambitious sales growth target for the upcoming financial year.

The CEO knew that his team had little chance of achieving this new stretch target, unless he did something significant about its collaborative culture. He initially focused his attention on just two of his direct reports. However, I advised him that singling out the head of Sales and the head of Marketing alone and making the change solely about these two individuals was not going to lead to the desired result.

By making the change about the organization's customers and their experience at every touch pint really rallied everyone together for a common cause and purpose. It moved everyone away from asking: Who's fault is it? to How can we do better as a team?

And the customers love the fresh new experience, too.

Chapter Takeaway

These are just some of my clients' success stories.

If you would like to see more client success stories, please visit peterstrohkorb.com/testimonials

Chapter 14:
Prevention is Better Than Cure

So far, we have only spoken about curing a pre-existing condition, i.e. applying Smarketing to help sales and marketing teams to improve their mutual support.

There is, however, an additional reason for organizations to deploy Smarketing: to prevent collaborative issues from becoming a challenge in the first place.

The challenges surrounding poor Smarketing develop as businesses grow and as the teams become more dispersed, both geographically and organizationally. There is really no sense in waiting for the challenge to occur only to then attempt to fix it after the fact. There is, however, a lot to be said about heading off a potential business challenge in the early stages of its growth.

As a business grows, Smarketing helps to put the elements in place to put it on the right track right from the start. One of our clients is an Australian arm of a global not-for-profit organization. Their new CEO came to us wanting the business to become more commercially sustainable. We joked that they had hitherto perhaps taken the term "not-for-profit" a bit too literally.

While conducting our Smarketing Opportunity Analysis, we discovered that the organization had been getting by without any real marketing to speak of.

When we started to take a closer look, it became clear that the same was true of the sales function.

Most of the organization's past success had come from the heroic efforts of a small number of individuals. There was no cohesive planning or strategy in place, and it did not appear that there ever had been. As we discovered, the prevailing attitude of the staff was: "We work for a not-for-profit organization, so we don't do any selling around here."

The CEO agreed with our findings and liked what we had uncovered in the Opportunity Assessment phase, and she decided to go ahead with rolling out Smarketing across the organization. We implemented the method in a combination of online and face to face sessions and were able to complete the project within a seven-month time frame, including the 360 Degree Opportunity Assessment and Smarketing implementation itself.

Right from the start, the method helped them come to grips with which collateral they already had in contrast to what they needed. We then helped them to understand how they could better support each other and build a more sustainable not-for-profit business.

The CEO made sure that Smarketing built on her foundations of an effective organizational structure, updated job descriptions and a new incentive scheme. This combination proved extremely effective in turning the business around and putting it on a commercially sustainable footing.

As we all know, an ounce of prevention is worth a pound of cure, and this is nowhere truer than in the world of collaborative enterprise. Organizations that find themselves in strong expansion mode and those that are about to open sales offices that are geographically separated from head office are strongly encouraged to consider leveraging Smarketing pro-actively.

Chapter Takeaway

You can now build Smarketing into the DNA of your business, if you plan for it.

Those who apply Smarketing preventatively as their business is growing are bound to avoid major problems down the track, when they are much harder to rectify.

So, decide to implement Smarketing and use it as your blueprint for sustainable business growth and ongoing success.

You see, prevention **is** better than a cure.

Peter Strohkorb

Chapter 15:
Over to You Now, A Call to Action

Even though this chapter is the last in the book, it is perhaps the most important in terms of the messages that I wanted to send out when I decided to write this book.

For a variety of reasons, many organizations procrastinate when it comes to making decisions, particularly when those decisions involve financial investment and/or are accompanied by any kind of change. Many executives seem to think that by delaying the "go" decision they delay spending and risk. Those who delay forget that there is significant opportunity risk and cost in doing nothing.

Below are some points for you to consider when you are facing an important decision in your business life. Each of these has an inherent dollar value associated with them. As you will see, sitting on your hands may well be more expensive than taking action:

- Clinging to inefficient business processes is wasteful

- Delaying the realization of business benefits is not smart

- Muddling through with the status quo is not innovative

- Getting by with quick fix 'Band-Aid' solutions is unsustainable

- Accepting an atmosphere of mutual blame and finger-pointing that leads to poor staff morale is unproductive

- Leaving the corporate sales know-how and the modus operandi of your top sales performers solely in their heads without leveraging it to improve your average sales performers is foolish

In contrast, Smarketing is a concept that is very easy to understand and is easy to implement, as long as you are open to change.

Do not fall victim to the seven most dangerous words in business. They are:

"We have always done it this way."

There is another saying. Ironically, this one is often attributed to Albert Einstein, one of the most brilliant minds ever: "Doing the same thing and expecting a different result is the definition of insanity."

Yes, Smarketing requires change. Change that is designed to lift sales revenue, profitability, staff engagement and customer satisfaction by showing Sales and Marketing teams how to better support each other. It is the right decision for today's forward-thinking organizations.

And: Leadership is about making good decisions and carrying them through to success.

But, Smarketing is not just good for business. It also presents a huge personal career opportunity.

So, if you are the Head of Sales or Marketing then what better way to demonstrate your leadership prowess to your CEO and to the

Executive Team, than to publicly take the lead to introduce Smarketing into your organization?

Rather than being defeatist with: "It is what it is.", There is nothing you can do about it.", "It's not the right time right now.", or any words to that effect, why not grab this unique opportunity to shine and to lift your organization as well as your professional profile with both hands, stand up for yourself and proclaim that, for the good of the organization and everyone it, you are the one who is willing to take positive and proactive action.

You then openly invite your counterpart in Sales or in Marketing to join you in taking on this important initiative with you!

Such a statement will establish you as a man or a woman of conviction and it will present you as not just a manager, but as a real leader.

Think about it: What could such a move do for you, for your professional brand and reputation, and ultimately for your career?

Please go ahead and ask for my help, advice, and guidance.

I will be there to support your success.

For example, we can work together to help introduce Smarketing into your organization, perhaps to win a specific pursuit, such as a "must-win" deal or a new key account. Or we can work together to review your sales funnel and to accelerate your sales pipeline.

Smarketing boils down to doing more with existing resources, providing a classical productivity boost to your two most customer-facing functions and to your sales funnel, resulting in sustainable sales revenue growth.

It may not quite be the same as "Do more with less.", but at the very least it is: "Do better with what you already have."

The outcome for you and your organization is likely to be higher win rates, elevated revenue and profits, more accurate forecasting, happier and more engaged employees, and more satisfied clients.

Who would not want to be associated with that sort of success?

Contact me for an initial private discussion about your specific situation and how I can help you discover how Smarketing can support your success, too.

Contact:

Email: pstrohkorb@peterstrohkorb.com

Website: peterstrohkorb.com

LinkedIn Profile: au.linkedin.com/in/peterstrohkorbsalesmarketing

Twitter: twitter.com/pstrohkorb

Webinars: brighttalk.com/channel/14325/

YouTube: youtube.com/channel/UCxZBIYubjdCk7zyQmcT8HgQ

About the Author

With more than 20 years' experience in B2B Sales and Marketing positions with some of the largest corporations on the planet, such as SONY, 3M, Canon, CSC and Dell, Peter Strohkorb has a history of successfully advising businesses of all sizes on how to grow their sales performance and lift revenue.

His specialization is designing, building, and implementing modern and effective sales processes for organizations in the B2B Technology, IT and Services sector across USA, ANZ and UK.

Peter Strohkorb now offers you Smarketing, his structured Sales and Marketing Productivity framework to help your Sales and your Marketing resources to work together more effectively, to drive sales revenue growth, to enhance your customer experience, and to lift your employee experience and engagement.

As an acclaimed speaker, presenter and specialist in his field, Peter has featured in the media internationally and has presented on three continents.

He is a Non-Executive Board Director, sitting on several company and advisory boards.

Peter holds tertiary qualifications in Marketing and Management from the prestigious Macquarie Graduate School of Management (MGSM) in Sydney, Australia.

Peter is available to work with you and your teams globally, be it online or in person.

He is looking forward to hearing from you.

www.ingramcontent.com/pod-product-compliance
Lightning Source LLC
Chambersburg PA
CBHW071403210526
45465CB00001B/229